I Don't look back in
Anger

Caroline Hughes Myers

Bloomington, IN   authorHOUSE™   Milton Keynes, UK

AuthorHouse™
1663 Liberty Drive, Suite 200
Bloomington, IN 47403
www.authorhouse.com
Phone: 1-800-839-8640

AuthorHouse™ UK Ltd.
500 Avebury Boulevard
Central Milton Keynes, MK9 2BE
www.authorhouse.co.uk
Phone: 08001974150

This book is a work of non-fiction. Unless otherwise noted, the author and the publisher make no explicit guarantees as to the accuracy of the information contained in this book and in some cases, names of people and places have been altered to protect their privacy.

First published by AuthorHouse 6/12/2006

ISBN: 1-4259-2910-9 (sc)

Printed in the United States of America
Bloomington, Indiana

This book is printed on acid-free paper.

Acknowledgements.

This book is dedicated to all those who suffered during the events described and to my daughter Candida. I hope that it will give her the opportunity to understand the part of history her parents were caught up in.

At times, it has been particularly difficult to relive the experience, much of which I had blotted out. I cried many times remembering those who—sadly—did not survive.

A special thank you to my wonderful family—my dear Dad and Mum who never gave up on me as I pursued my dreams, my sisters Michelle, Lorraine and Dee and my brother John. Thank you also to my special friend, Gwen, who had such faith in me.

Thanks, of course, to my husband Christian, who gave me the confidence and encouragement I needed to finally put my battered notes into book format.

This book would never have been completed without the assistance and support of others, especially my dear friends Sam and Alec.

For their kind permission to use references to the BBC *World Service News*, I am grateful to Miles Palmer, Head of Business Development, BBC *World Service*. London.

I would also like to thank Mr Hamad Al Nuiami, Marketing Director for the Al Jazeera Channel in Qatar for assistance and permission to use Al Jazeera's information.

I hope and pray that, in my daughter's lifetime, the bitterness and hatred in the world will eventually end, bringing to a close a long era of bloodshed and misery.

Freedom from War: Harmony for people.

Introduction: Kuwait, 1989.

I remember the journey vividly to this day. I was still apprehensive, but curious. I had decided that if all failed I could always return home. Nothing ventured, nothing gained! After a very emotional farewell to my family, I anxiously boarded the Kuwait Airways flight. I was en route to the Arabian Gulf; to Kuwait, which is well-known for its oil reserves and its large petrochemical industry.

Sitting on the aircraft, I wondered what the hell I was doing. I cried for most of the flight, unsure and nervous about what lay ahead. I was dressed like a nun in a jacket, scarf and black trousers with my hair tied up. I had been offered a position as a Manager and Skin Care Cabine Specialist for a company that was in the process of opening the Byblos Centre, an upmarket store for the affluent. The premises were built on two levels, and offered designer labels, from clothes to world-renowned beauty products. It would be my job to train the Arabic female staff who worked in this section.

I had researched the customs and regulations of Kuwait, and knew that it was a 'dry' Muslim State, governed by Shari'a Law (Islamic Law) and that although the official language was Arabic, English was widely spoken. The Gulf is conservative in comparison with the West, so I needed to understand Arab culture, as well as knowing how to follow certain rules, to ensure that my new experience in Kuwait would be a pleasant one. Women should wear loose-fitting clothing. I knew that people would treat me with more dignity if I showed respect for their culture.

After the long, eight-hour flight, we finally descended and I caught my first glimpse of Kuwait; the view was like that of a magical fairyland with beautiful lights on many of the buildings. I gazed in wonder at all the unfamiliar sights, including the traditional Arabic dress, with women covered from head to toe in their Abayas (long black robes). I smelled the sweet scents of Arabic perfume and oils. The airport was very busy, and I noticed a large group of young Asian girls awaiting documents and medical certificates before going on to work as maids. I felt tired and physically sick at the uncertainty of my future, but was relieved to spot a driver holding a large board with my name on it as I walked through customs. As I was led to the car, the warm night air and humidity hit me and added to my lethargy.

Once in the car, however, the journey was amazing. I admired the impressive architecture as we passed building after building, including the incredible Kuwait Towers. Exotic palm trees lined the route, and the country's wealth was very apparent.

I was looking and feeling pretty dreadful by the time we finally arrived at a huge villa. With a swimming pool in the garden and a perimeter wall surrounded by beautiful lights, it reminded me of *Lifestyles of the Rich and Famous*. A welcome party had been arranged, and as I walked into the magnificent residence in my very reserved attire, I was surprised to see women wearing elegant designer cocktail dresses. It was a far cry from what I had imagined! Everyone was very friendly and welcoming.

Eventually, I was driven with some family members of my new boss to the Messilah Beach Hotel, which was to be my new home until my apartment was complete. Once settled in my room, I used the international line to telephone my family to let them know that I had arrived safely. I babbled on, telling them my news so far; describing the journey, my meeting with the family and even the dishes of fresh dates that were waiting for me on the table in my hotel room.

My new life had started.

*

In time, I fell into the jet set lifestyle. I met many new friends at sailing parties and even enjoyed parties in the desert, with Arabic tents, camels and open fires. The parties, wherever they were held, had to be very discreet in order to avoid problems with the police. It was important to respect the laws of the country. One of the laws was that every resident must have an ID card linked to the details of their sponsor, with their address, date of birth, contact number and fingerprints. It was essential that the ID card be kept on the person at all times and produced on demand. To be found without the card was a very serious offence. On the whole, it was a system that worked well. As a single female, there were inevitably certain restrictions, but if rules were followed and the culture was respected, there were few problems. Life in Kuwait was getting better and better. It was exciting and very rewarding.

Unfortunately, it all came to a brutal, abrupt end in the early hours of 2nd August 1990 when Iraqi troops crossed the border, invading Kuwait and calling it the nineteenth Province of Iraq.

Kuwait. Wednesday 1st August 1990.

The political situation concerning Kuwait and neighbouring Iraq had become serious. Iraq claimed that Kuwait was exceeding its oil quota from an oilfield on the Iraq-Kuwait border. The local Arabic newspapers maintained that negotiations had been successful between the Kuwaiti ruling Al Sabah family and President Saddam Hussein, and that there was basically no cause for concern. We were not unduly worried.

Unfortunately, we did not have access to the international news, which was clearly showing a build-up of Iraqi troops on the Kuwaiti border. My family had telephoned days before, urging me to come home as the political plight appeared to be serious.

I had insisted that everything was fine and that if an invasion was likely, we would have been advised by the British Embassy to leave. So far, we had received no such warning.

My partner Chris and I sat on the beach with friends and their children. The obvious topic of conversation was Kuwait and Iraq. We frivolously discussed escape plans in the event of Iraq invading Kuwait, not thinking for one instant it would happen. As the evening ended, we sat watching the beautiful sunset with not a care in the world. What would tomorrow bring?

We were unaware that reconciliation talks between Iraq and Kuwait in the Saudi City of Taif had abruptly ended with Iraq storming out of the meeting. The Emir of Kuwait and his cabinet had fled to Saudi Arabia.

Thursday 2nd August 1990.

I awoke to a loud boom, followed by a series of disturbing noises that sounded like warfare. The vibrations echoed in the apartment block. My two terrified cats started frantically running around the bedroom, howling and climbing up the blinds in an effort to hide. I screamed at Chris that the Iraqis had invaded. He pulled himself up on the bed and looked at me bemusedly. We both rushed to the telephone, only to find that there was no ring tone. It was the same story with the radio and television. Fear slowly crept over us. Looking over the balcony of our fifth floor apartment, we could see the total chaos of the situation. Smoke was rising across the city from burnt out buildings. Cars and vehicles were all desperately trying to leave Kuwait, heading towards the Saudi Border with luggage and furniture falling off as horns blared. We clung to each other, with no idea what lay in store for us.

"I think we should get dressed," Chris said in deceptively calm tones. Sobbing and in total panic I grabbed my sandals, light skirt and jacket. Chris picked up his briefcase and I managed to get hold of my passport and one bag that contained some contractual papers. I was fortunate to actually have my passport, as many companies held on to them, requiring them to issue exit visas so that employees could leave the country.

Crying and completely bewildered, I began to worry about my cats, Flash and Mush (short for Mushkilah, an Arabic phrase meaning 'problem').

"For God's sake!" Chris shouted at me, finally losing his calm. "We may be killed and you want to worry about the bloody *cats*?" We decided that once we were able to assess the situation, we would deal with the cats. For now, they would have to stay locked in the apartment with plenty of food and water.

We lived in a district of Kuwait called "Salmiya." It was a predominantly Arabic residential area, central and close to all the chaos. Our Palestinian neighbours came and told us to leave and find shelter. We still hadn't received any warning from the British Embassy, but in total panic and disbelief, Chris decided that our best plan was to get to the Messilah Beach Hotel where he was the Food and Beverage Manager. Terrified, we scrambled into the car to drive to the hotel in the south-east of the city. We desperately hoped that there would be other Europeans there, and that they would know more about what was going on. The General Manager of the hotel was British and a warden for the British Embassy, so if anyone had any information, it would be him.

The fifteen minute journey seemed to last an eternity. The highways were jammed with cars. Many of them bulged with families, their worldly belongings strapped to the rooftops. The fear on people's faces and the children crying combined to resemble a scene from a film. Tempers flared as cars tried desperately to leave Kuwait via the Saudi border. Ironically, just the night before, we had declared that Kuwait would be totally incapable of withstanding a major attack.

We passed the beautiful Water Towers. They were still erect, almost in defiance. It was clear that they were badly damaged, but the famous revolving restaurant was still rotating. It wasn't long before military transport rolled into view. Chris told me to keep my head down, as we didn't want to attract any unwelcome attention. Tanks and soldiers armed with weapons, mostly Kalashnikovs, were everywhere. Helicopters hovered overhead. I prayed and prayed that we would arrive at the hotel before the soldiers in dark green tunics—some so young that they looked like children—stopped us. Chris did his best to keep us calm, and it was with immense relief that we arrived safely. The Iraqi soldiers had not yet managed to surround the hotel, but we realised that it would only be a matter of time before they did. We met our friends, John and Sarah, and their children, four year old Aisha and two year old Noura. John is British and had the position of Financial Controller at the Messilah Beach Hotel. His wife Sarah is from Egypt.

We were advised to hide in our friends' apartment on the hotel premises. Once there, I sat shaking uncontrollably, still crying. The shock and realisation of what was happening was difficult to absorb. Chris tried to calm Sarah and me down and we pulled ourselves together for long enough to attempt to make light of the horrendous situation for the children's sake. Their apartment was on ground level, like all the rooms in the hotel. The curtains were drawn, so the room was in darkness with only slithers of daylight shining through the open slits. We tried to look through the gaps in the curtain to see if we could establish what was going on. Outside, we could see truckloads of Iraqi soldiers, although they had not yet infiltrated the grounds of the hotel. We could hear the dreadful loud noises of bombing and gunfire.

The local television news informed us that the fairy-tale land of Kuwait was being destroyed and that law and order no longer existed. The Iraqis were looting and damaging anything in their way; raping, shooting and holding executions. They had overrun the country. We had been told by the Arabic hotel staff that, early in the morning, some Iraqi soldiers entered a Chinese restaurant, shot the men and raped the beautiful, innocent girls from the Philippines who worked there, before killing them, too. There were many other stories of brutality and we were incapable of stopping the carnage. Chris, like so many others, tried to call our parents to let them know we were alive and okay, but the international lines were down.

The General Manager decided it would be safer for us all to hide in the hotel basement. Periodically, we ran for cover through the hotel grounds with the children, trying to turn it into a fun game like hide-and-seek, when the bombing and shooting came closer. The Arabic hotel staff came regularly with food and soft drinks and kept us informed of the situation outside. My passport had been put in the hotel safe, along with the others. The hours seemed to last forever. Finally, the British Embassy managed to get the message through that an evacuation plan was to be put in place.

Meanwhile, the airport had been taken over and a British Airways flight that stopped for refuelling on its journey to Malaysia had been surrounded by Iraqi soldiers. The passengers were put on buses and displaced to various hotels around town. Some came to the Messilah Beach Hotel. While all of this was going on, the hotel staff managed to get a radio tuned into the BBC *World Service*. This became our lifeline to the world outside.

At times like these, one cannot but think of one's loved ones and how they must be distraught at seeing the events unfolding. My Irish family is a wonderful, close–knit unit. I remembered that when I was offered the position in Kuwait, my father had thought it would be a fantastic opportunity for me to sample another country and to experience the customs and culture. Until then, I had never even heard of Kuwait and I remember my dad showing me where it was on a world map. My initial reaction had been surprise at how close it was to Iran. My dad, being his usual philosophical self, had said, "Go for it, Caroline. You can always return home if it all goes wrong." My mother had had more reservations, but I had managed to convince myself that this was to be a new chapter in my life, and that it would be an exciting new challenge.

Now, I found that the more I thought about my sisters and brother, the more emotional I became.

The most painful memory of the first ten hours in the hotel was the unmistakable fear on the men's faces, despite their best attempts to conceal it. Our lives had already changed so dramatically from peace, sunshine and freedom to a living nightmare. What could my family be thinking? They had no idea where their daughter was, or even if she was still alive. My tears flowed freely, imagining their distress.

Friday 3rd August 1990.

By Friday, everyone had been taken to the hotel basement for safety, including paying guests, some passengers from the British Airways flight and families of the staff. The Arabic staff felt that the basement would shelter us from the heavy bombing and persistent noise of gunfire. They were all wonderful in such fearful circumstances.

Unable to sleep, we sat through the night, huddling together and planning escape routes. While these were totally unrealistic, it was a great morale boost. By now, the hotel basement resembled a fallout shelter from a film about World War One. People were crying, some hysterically, at the realisation that we were prisoners in the hotel. The constant noise of explosions and gunfire made everyone nervous, and even the sound of someone opening a can of fizzy drink made me jump in fear. The Arabic hotel staff continued to relay information about the military presence outside. Until now, the Iraqi soldiers had remained outside the perimeter of the hotel, but this simply gave us a false sense of security.

It's amazing how your life appears to pass in front of you when you are faced with the fear and real possibility of dying. You regret not having had time—or *made* time—in your life to achieve your dreams. When I saw the fear in the men's faces, I realised that perhaps we would not be lucky enough to survive. Chris held me in his arms, trying to reassure me by saying that we would be evacuated.

The basement was becoming claustrophobic. There were people sitting on the floor, and all one could hear was the constant noise of sobbing, and obviously frightened parents trying to entertain their children. The men felt totally useless and powerless.

After a while, Sarah wanted to go back to their apartment to retrieve some possessions, so at about three in the morning we all decided to try to go back. We agreed to get out of the basement and run through the grounds, hiding behind palm trees and ducking at the sudden sound of gunfire in the distance. Eventually, we reached the apartment and quickly entered, locking the door. Thank God, we had a radio that we could tune into the BBC *World Service News*. Messages via the radio were now informing British residents to stay where they were until an update on evacuation plans was in place. The Arabic staff continued to relay stories of desperate citizens trying to get into the British Embassy, only to be turned away for security reasons. That was when people decided to fend for themselves and go into hiding.

*

Inside the apartment, we drew the curtains so as not to attract attention from the soldiers. When the children were asleep, we discussed the situation. We were convinced the Embassy would have an evacuation plan and somehow march in and rescue everyone. We talked and talked, sometimes nodding off only to be awoken by the loud bangs and gunfire. Once in a while, we opened a little slit in the curtains to see the night sky alight with tracer bullets. We were so scared that someone would see the curtain twitching we took turns to sit on the floor to get a glimpse of the bright sky.

Although we were in a life and death situation, I kept crying about the cats. I imagined them starving to death in the apartment. I love animals. So much so, that some people might see it as a weakness! I always used to feed the local strays, and I couldn't bear simply to abandon my own cats. Early in the morning, the hotel staff rang Sarah on the internal telephone and told her that a ceasefire was in place and that it was safe to venture out for emergency provisions. I knew that the cats were in the apartment, and that I also had five thousand pounds Sterling there. I had been saving the money since my arrival in Kuwait, hidden in a pair of tights in a suitcase. The money tipped the balance when it came to persuading Chris to agree that we should return to our apartment for the cats. Of course, only an animal person would understand this need. Chris understood, even though in hindsight it was totally ridiculous. People do the strangest things under stress. Chris decided to venture outside the hotel grounds, still surrounded by soldiers, with checkpoints everywhere and armed soldiers stopping and searching vehicles. He managed to get to Salmiya and our apartment. The devastation in and around the city of Kuwait was a total shock to him and clear proof that we really were in a war zone; buildings were still smouldering. The destruction of all the beautiful landmark buildings and the broken glass, burnt-out cars and property strewn across the pavements was terrible. Luckily for us and the cats, the Iraqi soldiers had not reached our building yet. Chris managed to get to the apartment block without any problems. Terrified, he ran to the apartment and, once inside, grabbed the cats and a suitcase already packed for our trip home, not forgetting the saved money. We didn't have a cat basket, so the cats went into a box until they got to the car. Once inside the vehicle, the terrified animals scratched their way out.

Chris started to head back to the hotel, with the cats running around the car, mewing like mad things. When Chris approached a checkpoint, the soldiers gestured him to stop. Chris, convinced that this was it, opened the window. The soldier abruptly asked him for his ID card. As he produced it, the soldier noticed the cats running around the car howling. Luckily for Chris, he was so surprised by this sight that he merely told him to move on.

Back at the hotel, we were painfully aware that it had been two hours since Chris left. By now, we were frantic and starting to fear the worst. Fortunately, he arrived back safely, but he was quite shaken by the experience. John said that I was probably the only person with money, because all the bank services had been stopped and the cash stolen; maybe we would able to turn this to our advantage.

Aisha and Noura were very excited about the cats. Sarah, not being a cat lover, was not so impressed but, nevertheless, they stayed with us in the apartment. We couldn't let them out, so the bath became the cats' toilet, much to Sarah's disgust. The Arabic hotel staff came to the room with food, but no one could eat much as we were all so numb with fear. By now, our mental and physical well being had started to deteriorate. Sarah and I had periodic bouts of diarrhoea, so after a few hours Sarah made lemonade with egg white to try and stop it. It worked for a short period, but the taste made me feel rather nauseous. All the while, the constant noise of bombing and gunfire appeared to be getting closer, vibrations echoing around the apartment block.

Before too long, we decided it was no longer safe to stay in the apartment, so we moved to another room, at the rear of the hotel. Once again, we ran between the palm trees in the hotel grounds with the children. The fear of being raped was always on my mind. The men were terrified for us, but we had been told that an evacuation plan would soon be instigated and that we should stay put. We considered trying to escape to the Saudi border in a car, but decided that that might be foolish, especially with two small children. We would wait for the evacuation. Stories emerged about Iraqi soldiers capturing European civilians in a place called "Ahmadi", where there had been a British military base. Apparently, the men had been taken away by force. Where, no one knew. The soldiers had forcefully entered one couple's apartment, so the husband told his wife to lock herself in the bedroom. They opened the door with brute strength and two soldiers held the husband while three or more raped and humiliated his wife. Men wanted to protect their wives and children by going into hiding. Most of the Iraqi soldiers were conscripts; some wore only torn sandals on their feet, clearly having never seen such wealth as is abundant in Kuwait. Iraq was still recovering from the hardship and poverty of the war with Iran. All over Kuwait city, the looting seemed to have some sort of order; expensive cars were all on the road to Baghdad, along with trucks full of food and electrical items. You name it, it was on trucks heading towards Iraq. Some of the high-ranking Iraqi officers tried to maintain some law and order, as Kuwait was in a state of total anarchy. There were stories of Iraqi officers executing their own men for some of their crimes. We also heard nightmarish accounts of horrendous brutality towards the Kuwaiti people who were left behind. Torture chambers had been set up and fathers and sons executed for trying to protect their loved ones. Kuwait had become a living hell.

During the night, the Iraqi soldiers surrounding the Messilah Beach Hotel finally started to infiltrate the hotel grounds. It was obvious that we were no longer safe as the soldiers moved slowly in and around the grounds, blocking every conceivable exit. By now, we were inconsolable; Sarah and I cried and prayed for a solution. I remember Aisha asking why I was always crying, to which we answered that I had an allergy that made my eyes water. The Arabic staff continued to telephone on the internal phone and converse with Sarah in Arabic about the location of the soldiers. We were told that under no circumstances should we females be seen.

<u>Saturday 4th August 1990.</u>

The staff told us that the Iraqis were allowing people to venture out for emergency provisions, so with their confirmation that it would be okay, Chris and John decided to go for supplies, such as nappies for Noura, cigarettes and tampons. I also remember the girls pleading for chocolate. We hugged each other and prayed for their safe return.

The shopping expedition didn't go according to plan. Chris and John were captured and taunted at gunpoint, never to return to the hotel.

The men had left us at about ten o'clock in the morning. A few hours later, Sarah and I started to panic. Exhausted from crying, we just knew something was very wrong. Sarah called reception to try and get some information about their whereabouts, but without luck. We knew that something dreadful must have happened. We were so terrified and felt so very vulnerable that we barricaded ourselves and the children in the room for fear of being taken by the Iraqi soldiers and raped.

By now, the military presence around the hotel was immense; a living nightmare. We were defenceless and utterly reliant on the help of others.

Food was left outside the door at strategic times when the soldiers were not in sight, and we had to quickly open the door and grab the tray of food. So far, we had not been seen. The girls were becoming restless from being locked in a room with curtains drawn and little daylight coming through. By now, Sarah and I had come to accept that Chris and John were probably dead and that we must remain strong for the girls and survive as best we could.

Sunday 5th August 1990.

Sarah and I had succumbed to despair. We spent our time huddling together crying and drifting in and out of sleep, while we tried to be rational about our circumstances. On Sunday, we woke from a disturbed sleep at around five in the morning, but there was still no news. The General Manager had nothing to report and we waited anxiously, imagining the worst. At eleven we were told that Chris and John had been transferred to Basra, near the Iraqi border. They were alive, but God help us, what would we do now? What on earth were they doing in Basra? They were innocent men who had gone out for some emergency provisions. We had to be strong, if only for the children's sake, but it was very difficult. We talked about all of us eventually getting out of this mess and having a reunion in London with our husbands; those idiots who had left us all alone in this bloody awful situation!

Everyone in the hotel was very tense. There were soldiers everywhere and we were frightened to death. The worst was our fear of the unknown.

"We've got to go," Sarah said finally. "I want to go to Salhir, nearer Kuwait city." I knew she was crazy. The only way to dissuade her was to shout and be firm. Fortunately, it worked. But then she said that we should go by car to Basra with an Arabic friend, and get out through a border.

Sunday was an awful, long day. We were unable to eat, or indeed do much other than cry, and occasionally laugh and talk about dreams for the future. Time seemed to stand still. We were angry with the men for leaving us. Sometimes we talked about them in the past tense, unsure as to whether they were alive. We tried to imagine the horrors they might be facing if they were still alive and wondered how they would handle the events, mentally and physically. We sat glued to the television; Sarah translated the news showing Iraqi troops leaving Kuwait City and arriving to great cheers from their people in Basra. Unfortunately, many troops stayed behind in Kuwait. The television persistently showed news from the new Iraqi regime, claiming their new province and mentioning that captured civilian men had been transferred to Baghdad. Total hysteria overcame us as we thought of Chris and John being the next European hostages and we started to joke about how we would appeal on international television for their release. We had to force ourselves to laugh, just to boost our confidence and make us smile.

"Let's move to a safer room," I finally suggested, "further away from all the activity." Sarah agreed, so we took essential items and, when the coast was clear at night, ran around the palm trees to what we thought was a safer room, begging with the children to be silent. We were petrified, but managed to reach the rooms at the far end of the hotel without being detected. The hotel was cloaked in an eerie silence; there was no movement other than that of the armed soldiers.

Monday 6th August 1990.

After yet another night of disturbed sleep, I woke in the early hours to the sound of knocking on the door. Sarah was hysterical as she came from the bathroom, while I went to try and see who was there.

"Don't open it!" Sarah whispered frantically. I nodded in answer; I knew not to open the door; the soldiers were still everywhere. I opened the curtain slightly and gaped in total disbelief. The grounds of the hotel were surrounded. I closed the curtain and stood shaking and crying as the knocking continued. Speaking in Arabic, Sarah discovered that it was two staff from reception with a food tray, telling us that the situation was desperate and that we should stay put. They told us to lock the door and not to open it unless it was them. They couldn't guarantee our safety for much longer. The main reception area had been taken over by Iraqi officers as their local headquarters.

At quarter past eight, the phone rang and Sarah answered. The conversation was in Arabic and, as it progressed, Sarah's face grew very pale and displayed horror. In my heart, I knew that the conversation was about me. An Iraqi officer had given the message that the "British girl with Sarah" must go immediately to reception. I collapsed on the floor in shock and the tears began again. Sarah sat on the floor, hugging me. I'll never forget the fear in her eyes.

"I'll hide you!" she said, but there was nowhere and we had no men to protect us. The penalty for hiding Europeans was death, so it was unfair to even hope that she could, especially as she had two small children. It seemed my time had finally come; at least, as an Egyptian, Sarah had some hope. She begged me not to mention Aisha and Noura to the Iraqi officials, as they had British passports. Because she had travelled so much with her husband John, Sarah had never spent enough time in the UK to apply for one for herself.

Now that a decision was made, Sarah became anxious.

"Hurry!" she said. "It will make things worse if you are slow." She put a few items of clothing into a small canvas bag and tied my hair up in a ponytail. I was still wearing Chris' baggy blue shirt and tracksuit bottoms.

"Put on sunglasses as well," Sarah advised me. "You'll attract less unwelcome attention that way." She was so scared for me. I hugged and kissed the frightened girls as they wept. Sarah shouted at them to be quiet and told them she would be back soon. She locked them in the room along with the cats, telling me that she would care for the animals. Outside the apartment door, there were armed soldiers. I will never forget the way they looked at us as we walked arm-in-arm, mute with terror. As we approached the main reception, we saw an old green military bus parked nearby with the curtains drawn. Sarah held my hand and reminded me of my promise not to mention the girls. Unable to speak, I just nodded. We slowly walked through the door of the reception area that now resembled something from a war film. There was a desk set up in the corner surrounded by what looked like high-ranking Iraqi military.

The officer who, to judge from his uniform and his authoritarian manner, appeared to be in command, came over and asked my nationality. I was unable to speak as I was sobbing so much, so Sarah answered for me.

He said that the British government had advised that Kuwait was no longer a safe place for British nationals and that we would be taken to a safe destination. He showed me my passport, which had been taken from the hotel safe. The hotel staff had been forced to disclose the whereabouts of Europeans; that was how they knew where people were. The desk had many papers, arranged in different piles.

"Sign your name and write down your nationality here," the Iraqi official ordered me, but I was shaking so much that I had to steady my right hand with the left before I could even manage a scribble. He explained that Sarah would be well looked after and that her country would be making plans to evacuate their nationals.

Sarah and I clutched each other in the corridor as the soldiers asked me to get on the bus. Shaking and twitching in fear, I walked towards the old green bus, holding my bag and Chris' briefcase. I had little choice but to comply with their orders. An armed soldier escorted me onto the bus, leaving a sobbing Sarah behind. I will never forget the terrified expression on her face.

As I entered the bus, through my tears I could see other Europeans sitting in silence, fear written on their faces. In total, there were about twenty to twenty five of us; men, women and children. I sat two seats from the front. Fortunately, one of the chefs from the hotel, Ian, came and sat beside me. In my tears and confusion, I couldn't really see who was there, but Ian's presence made me feel a lot safer. The two armed Iraqi soldiers sat at the front with the driver. The heat on the bus was stifling, as the temperature outside was a hundred and fifteen degrees and the air-conditioning units were not working. Above my head were reminders of the war; army berets and old army boots. Even my feet rested on yet more army boots. Ian joked that we should keep them as a souvenir. The bus had obviously been used to transport soldiers into Kuwait from the Iraqi border.

The bus journey started at about half past nine in the morning. The bewildered hotel staff who remained behind watched the bus depart with fear in their eyes. Everyone appeared calm, although they were probably just numb from the events of the past few days. The soldiers at the front of the bus sat talking and joking in Arabic, but the uncanny silence surrounding us was scary, as we had no idea where we were going. We were only able to see through a slit in the curtains.

We travelled through Kuwait city, passing the badly damaged water towers. The roads seemed to have survived most of the damage, but wrecked cars remained abandoned. Many walls had collapsed when tanks had forced their way in. The Crown Prince's Palace was still standing, surrounded by broken glass and rubble. Hotels were damaged and complete floors were destroyed. Armed soldiers in military tanks covered the coast of the Gulf to the Messilah Beach Hotel; tents had been set up and soldiers could be seen washing in the sea. Also visible were other Arab nationals in their traditional white *thobes,* brandishing weapons. This was a disturbing sight, as they had the freedom to inform on those in hiding and terrorise the innocent people left behind.

In Kuwait City, gunfire and explosions shattered the peace we had once enjoyed. The other nationals were calling themselves "The People's Army." They were mostly teenagers with revenge on their minds, armed and freely roaming the streets. Anarchy reigned.

*

By now, we realised that we were heading for Basra on the Southern Iraqi border. After an hour or so, the terrible dry desert heat became unbearable. There was an awful smell of stale sweat from our terrified bodies. Periodically, soldiers would walk up and down the bus handing out water and 7 UP. An hour into the journey, the bus came to a sudden stop at a checkpoint and the soldiers left the bus, only for different ones to enter. They walked up and down, staring at us. Ian told me to keep my head down and not to look at them. After a few minutes, they left the bus. Confused and unsure as to what was going on, we sat in absolute silence. At the time, I thought they were going to machine gun the bus and kill us all. It would have been quite easy to do, an ideal opportunity with no one to help or protect us. I suffered another unquenchable outburst of tears as I thought of my family and the plans Chris and I had shared. I was convinced that if he was not dead, he could be maimed or held for years as a hostage, like some in Beirut.

Behind us, we could see two more buses holding Europeans. We could only assume they were the rest of the unfortunate people on the British Airways flight. In front, we could see trucks being emptied of valuables, looted from Kuwait by the soldiers; gold, cigarettes, electrical goods and more.

We continued the journey for another couple of hours, still in silence. Occasionally, the children on the bus would try to play "I spy" with their parents, who endeavoured to keep them calm. Eventually we arrived at the Basra border. A few locals were staring at us, so we were asked to keep the curtains drawn to prevent any confrontation. A sign informed us that it was forty kilometres to Basra centre.

Around us, we could see a dry, desolate land with wild dogs roaming freely; sand and still more sand. The bus stopped once again outside what looked like a prison camp and the soldiers got off for about forty-five minutes. The camp was a very old building with ancient, rusty bars on the windows. We all thought the worst. We waited, anticipating our fears. Even if they did kill us, how could they possibly kill innocent children? After what seemed like an eternity, the soldiers got back on the bus and we drove off, as they conversed in Arabic. Ian was sweating profusely, so I found an old shirt in my bag and he used it for wiping his face and neck.

At half past two, we arrived at the Basra Sheraton Hotel with a mixture of shock, relief and confusion. In total, ninety-one people on three buses had left Kuwait that morning. We were escorted off the bus and told to go to the reception. The sun shone on the fantastic statues of soldiers—all with guns apparently pointing towards Iran—surrounding the Shatt Al Arab Seaway that flows into the Arabian Gulf. Tired, exhausted and with stomach cramps, I entered the hotel.

The message the Iraqi soldiers gave us then was impossible to believe; we would be given a key to a hotel room to shower and then we would have some lunch. After that, we would be taken to a destination of our choice. It was difficult to comprehend and I was more than a little suspicious. But we had no control over the situation; we just followed the rules and hoped and prayed that we were being told the truth. I was terrified when a male member of staff told me to follow him. We went into a lift and took it to the fourth floor. There, he opened one of the rooms.

"Please," he said. "you have shower and then I will come back to take you downstairs for lunch." Once inside the room, I briefly felt some relief. I sat on the bed and sobbed my heart out. Then I was convinced the Iraqis were watching me; I could feel my paranoia taking over. Still, the bathroom was a great luxury. My stomach cramps had become unbearable and the diarrhoea had started again—and so, unexpectedly, had my period. I disposed of my soiled undergarments and quickly had a shower. I had no provisions for menstruation, so I had to improvise with toilet paper and hope that it would suffice until more suitable provisions were available. I put on another of Chris' shirts and baggy tracksuit bottoms, tied my hair up in a ponytail and sat on the bed looking in the mirror at my almost unrecognisable reflection as I tried to think clearly about recent events.

There was a sudden knock at the door; it was the same man as before.

"Follow me to the lift," he requested. I did, and he took me to a banqueting room containing a beautiful buffet.

"Maybe they really *will* let us go home," I thought for just a split second. Ian came over and we picked some food from the buffet, but everyone's appetite had long since diminished. I managed to eat some bread to try and stop the diarrhoea.

As well as the banquet, the bar was open and serving drinks.

"All I want to do is get blotto," Ian said, so we both sat at the bar ordering beer and gin and tonics, chain-smoking and reminiscing about Chris, John, Sarah and the girls. The guilt I felt about having left Sarah and the girls behind was terrible. Ian and I could drink as much as we liked, but it did not numb the pain or anguish we felt.

*

After about eight hours, an Iraqi official asked us to write down our names and nationalities before calling us into the foyer, which had been set up as an office. Iraqi military were sitting behind desks with sheets of paper bearing our details. Once in possession of our information, they segregated us into lines according to our nationalities and asked us to move forward and confirm name and nationality as we were called. The British were in one line and Americans in another with other nationalities such as the Australians joining the British. It was now about eleven and dark outside, yet still they insisted we would be going home. Before entering the buses, we went through the same procedure all over again. We were all confused and scared.

The buses had arrived at the forecourt of the hotel with their curtains drawn. Slowly, the harsh reality became more apparent. We were like sheep to the slaughter. We were instructed to listen for our names, confirm nationality and to go to the buses as instructed. In an orderly fashion, people listened for their names and started to board. It was obvious that the British and Americans were being separated.

*

On the bus, Ian and I sat together, wondering what was going to happen next, although I was just too numb to contemplate what lay in store. A short journey through the streets of Basra followed. In the darkness, we were driven to a railway station, which was surrounded by a huge military presence; military buses and armed uniformed soldiers.

We were most definitely not going home. Instead, we were escorted by the armed soldiers, still segregated by nationality, into different compartments on the military train. Ian went in front of me, whispering that I should follow him so we could stay together. As we entered, we saw armed soldiers standing along the aisle. As I tried to move past, keeping my head down, one large armed soldier pushed me into the side of the train, pushing his stale, sweaty body against me in the narrow aisle. Then he gave me an almighty thump on the back telling me to move in Arabic and waving his hands about. Ian turned around and looked on in shock as I carried on walking, petrified. We were shown into a compartment with four bunk beds, all covered with green military blankets. The doors and windows had holes from previous conflicts. Bullets were embedded in the metal. Together with us there were two middle aged ladies who had been unfortunate enough to have been on the BA flight. I climbed onto the top bunk and Ian went on the other. We were all too numb and frightened to speak.

I hid under the dirty green blanket in fear that the fat soldier would come back later to taunt me. I was desperate for the toilet, but too scared to venture out of the cabin. I kept convincing myself it was a question of mind over matter and that I didn't really need to go. The train moved off slowly. With my vivid imagination doing overtime, I convinced myself that they were going to gas us on the train. I prayed and hoped that, if this was true, it would be quick and would happen when we had fallen asleep from sheer exhaustion.

Once again, I cried myself to sleep.

Tuesday 7th August 1990.

A sudden loud bang on the door woke us. It was daylight and there was lots of noise and activity and shouting in Arabic. Thank God, we were still alive!

My mouth was dry, I had dreadful cramps from my period, and I needed the toilet desperately. Relieved to see daylight, we looked around at the grim surroundings and wondered to each other in whispers about what would happen next. The unmistakable stale smell of unwashed bodies was perceptible. I felt awful, dirty and tired. As we were all in the same situation, no one took any notice of hygiene. We just wanted to survive.

I had to go to the toilet so I looked out the compartment door anxiously. Other people were going, so I took a deep breath and ventured along the aisle. The soldiers were preoccupied with the commotion outside, so I quickly went to the toilet, changed the tissues and arrived back without incident. After our eleven-hour journey through the night, we were all defenceless. It was a disturbing to see men so pathetic and helpless, all too terrified to ask questions.

The soldiers came back on the train and told us to follow them. In our various groups, we slowly left the train in their wake. Head down, I walked behind Ian. Outside there was another array of buses, all with curtains on the windows. By now, the soldiers had our names and nationalities and we were asked to proceed onto the buses as before, with the people we had travelled with from Basra. Armed soldiers surrounded the railway station and the vehicles.

Too exhausted and numb to speak, we entered the buses in silence, escorted by four armed soldiers. *What next?* I wondered. It was highly unlikely that we were going home. As the journey began, we could see street signs displaying "Baghdad City, Iraq" through the slit in the curtains.

After twenty minutes or so, the bus came to a halt and once again we were asked to leave it. As we stepped off, the heat and bright sunshine hit me. It was like an oven door being opened and a bright camera flash going off. We were at what appeared to be a back tradesmen's entrance to a large building. It was the Hotel Al Mansour Melia. Its motto was "Tradition and Hospitality." The hotel was approved by the general directorate of tourism, but we were not tourists. We were escorted inside with armed guards, now in civilian clothes, lining the tradesmen's entrance. They were posted two to three yards apart.

Inside, we were shown into a huge banqueting room. Tables had been prepared for breakfast, and in the far corner there was even tea and coffee. The aroma was wonderful and again I briefly thought that maybe—just maybe—we really would go home. In the room, we discovered the British military men who had been taken from the camp in Ahmadi in Kuwait. As they had breakfast, they looked us all over, but they were at the other end of the room so we were unable to speak to them.

We were asked to sit down and given a form to complete, asking for more details such as our names, nationality, passport numbers, occupations in Kuwait and salary. After completing the form, the Iraqi English-speaking guard collected it from me and asked for my passport. We were told by a translator that a doctor was available if required. We all looked dreadful; tired and pale with red eyes from constant crying. Armed guards escorted us to the toilets, and I managed to get fresh tissues to keep me going until there were suitable provisions for menstruation. A lady with me had Chanel No.5 in her bag and, as our body odour was becoming even worse, we dabbed the perfume under our arms.

"That's the most expensive antiperspirant we'll ever use!" I said. We laughed, and left the toilets to be escorted back to the banqueting room. There, we were offered tea, coffee, bread and cereal. I still clung to the hope that we might go home, but when they took my passport I understood the reality. During breakfast, I tried to find out what had happened to Chris and John. As we walked to the far end of the room for tea, some of the British military men joined the queue, discreetly searching for information from us. One of them overheard me talking about Chris and John. It transpired that this man had been taken from Kuwait with them and that they were actually here, in the Mansour Melia!

Chris and I were finally reunited. Just after I heard this wonderful news, I turned around through a haze of tears, and there stood Chris and John. At first, I hardly recognised Chris. He was very pale and had three days' beard growth. With a vacant, expressionless face and sunken eyes framed by dark bags, he looked truly terrible. I stood dazed and unable to speak, with tears rolling down my cheeks. Eventually we both walked calmly towards each other, and clasped our arms tightly around one another. I was almost breathless from Chris' tight embrace. We said nothing for a while.

"What have they done to you?" Chris asked me then. "Did they hurt you?" I had forgotten how awful I must have looked, with my eyes still swollen from all the crying and fear written on my face. But we were still alive and that was all that mattered. So long as we were together, we would give each other strength and be better able to cope with whatever happened.

John waited for a few minutes and then, desperate for news of his family, he started to flood me with questions. He assumed Sarah and the girls were with me: "Where are they?" My guilt about having left them behind and memory of Sarah's desperate offer prompted my uncontrollable sobs. When I had calmed down, I explained as best I could the events of the last couple of days. I tried to convince John that Sarah was a strong, capable lady who would have the Arabic staff looking out for her and the girls. It was also true that the Iraqis were only interested in Europeans. The Iraqi officer at the Messilah Beach Hotel had reassured me that she would be looked after by her home country. I prayed that this was true and that in the not too distant future we would all be reunited and able to cry and laugh about this nightmare.

Then, an Iraqi armed guard came over and told me to go back to my table, so once again I was separated from Chris. At that point, a doctor finally came to see us. He was a very pleasant man who asked if we had any medical problems and if we were taking any medication for diabetes, heart problems etc. After about two hours, we were escorted by armed guards into a lift and up to the eighth floor. I was shown to a room and told to go in. Because I was terrified to go in on my own, Ian accompanied me, saying we were family. He was not very convincing, but they allowed us to go into the room together. Then, two Iraqi officials entered with a photographer. The official told me to sit on the bed and the photographer took my photograph. He changed cameras, and then took another one. Apparently one was in colour and one in black and white. Ian's photograph was also taken.

Things had veered from the sublime to the ridiculous; I would start to feel a little safer and then something bizarre would happen to make me wonder what the hell they were going to do with us. *Why did they want the photos?* My imagination was doing overtime yet again. The Iraqis left the room as abruptly as they had entered, closing the door behind them.

*

Ian and I looked around the luxurious room, which had a balcony overlooking Baghdad City. There were two single beds, a television that had been disconnected and a bathroom. I noticed that the telephones had been removed; obvious telephone cables protruded from the walls.

"If anyone asks us, we'll say that we are married," Ian and I agreed. Ian also felt safer being thought to be my husband rather than single. We were too scared to open the door so we just sat talking. Just then, I found a bottle of home-made red wine that Sarah must have slipped in my bag. At last, a reason to smile! Ian pushed the cork into the bottle while I found glasses in the bathroom.

"Let's drink to an end to this nightmare!" Ian said. We drank deeply. Convinced the rooms were bugged, we decided to sit on the balcony and talk about the last few days. Under the circumstances, the usually less than appetising home-brew tasted pretty good!

It was strange to think that everything we owned or had earned was still in Kuwait. All I had now was my bag, with a few clothes. All my photos of happier times in Kuwait had probably been torn or burned, along with all my lovely clothes. All our possessions were gone. But we were still alive, at least for now, so we were lucky. I wondered where my poor cats were.

Our peace was disturbed by a knock at the door. It was Chris, standing with two armed guards. He had persuaded the guards that we were married and, through translators, we explained that we had been separated in Kuwait and longed to be together. Ian was shocked but understanding.

*

Now I was concerned that if our captors discovered that we were not actually married, we might be used us an example. Chris and I decided to use my birthday date as our wedding day so we would both have the same date in our minds. After all, we were still in a Muslim country. Alone together at last, Chris was finally able to tell me the story of his journey to Baghdad. I held him and listened as he spoke.

John and Chris had been talking to a German who had been staying at the Messilah Beach Hotel. Paul had boasted about how many times he had left the hotel that morning and how little investigation he had been subjected to at Iraqi roadblocks. He also mentioned he had been to the Sultan Centre Supermarket, which was open for cigarettes. Upon hearing this news, John suggested going to the Sultan Centre for cigarettes, too. Chris was not convinced that three European guys, who didn't speak Arabic, should venture out, but he tentatively agreed, swayed by John's confidence. He still felt wary of leaving the hotel, mainly because if anything did happen, Sarah and I would have had no idea what was going on. They left the hotel and drove along the Gulf Road via one or two checkpoints. Tanks and armoured cars were dotted along the beach side of the road with all their guns pointing toward the ocean. Hundreds of Iraqi soldiers rested in small groups in shaded areas along the road. Just past the SAS hotel, they and another fifteen or twenty cars were turned back at a roadblock. They took the next u-turn off the Gulf Road to try another route to the Sultan Centre. Just off the road, they found a Haji shop where they stopped to buy cigarettes and a cold drink. Chris felt uneasy being out in the car. When they reached the Gulf Road Sultan Centre via the back streets, they found it closed, and made a quick decision to travel along the Fahaheel Expressway to Salmiya, to find out if the main Sultan Centre was open. There were no roadblocks along the expressway and a steady flow of traffic was evident. On arriving at the Sultan Centre in Salmiya, they were disappointed to discover that it was also closed. It was annoying; they had come this far without any problems only to find the shops closed! Then John said that, as they were already heading in the right direction, they should have a look along the Gulf Road. Once again, Chris was uneasy about being there, although the presence of what seemed like normal traffic eased his tension. They passed the Crown Prince's Sief Palace, blown to a mere shell of its previous elegance. By now, they were all intrigued and wanted to find out what other damage had been done. They knew that most of the resistance had taken place in the centre, close to the Emir's Palace.

They continued along the Gulf road, which was scattered with Iraqi tanks and groups of soldiers relaxing in the shade. After passing the Kuwait International Hotel, they looked at the Kuwait Towers for signs of damage. There had been rumours that they had been hit by missiles. There was some damage at the bases of the towers, but most had been caused by bullets smashing the windows of the restaurant and viewing deck. Just before actually reaching the Towers, all traffic was diverted back towards the Kuwait International Hotel. They assumed that this was to prevent them passing the Emiri Palace, where there might still have been some resistance. There seemed to be a much more organised military presence in the area. Almost in a daze, John continued driving towards the city centre, past two huge shell marks high up on the side of an apartment block. After passing some way behind the Emiri residence and the gold souks, they neared the city centre, where roadblocks became much more prevalent. John tried to avoid one, but was severely reprimanded by the soldiers and forced to reverse. They were asked to open the boot of the car. The soldiers found some barbecue charcoal. Confusion reigned for a few minutes until they managed to explain what it was for. They then travelled further into the city and stopped at a local cash point machine to try and withdraw some cash. It was empty.

They continued towards a large apartment block near the Meridian Hotel and on towards the Sheraton Hotel. In this area, there was much more military activity and Chris regretted not having suggested that they turn back earlier. They saw at least three buses that had been shot up, and tens of cars riddled with bullet holes; all deserted in the middle of the roundabout with their doors open.

By now, they were very worried, and agreed they should return to the Messilah Hotel as quickly as possible. At the roundabout, they took their exit and began heading towards the hotel until they came to another road block where they slowed up to a soldier checking papers. He asked if they were British and, following confirmation, he told them to pull over. By now, they were very concerned. John assumed they wanted to check the boot again, but Chris was sure they were in for it. John got out of the car and opened the boot while the soldier continued to check other cars, still holding their IDs. Then he summoned another soldier and pointed at John's car. This soldier walked over with his AK-47 machine gun, told John to get in the car, jumped in the back seat and told Chris to move over, pointing his gun at him. He told John to drive down the road towards an old Ministry building, where they were ordered out of the car. Another soldier took the car keys from John and locked it. They were then joined by another five soldiers who assured them that everything was fine. All three men were very concerned by now. Chris kept thinking about his family, and wondering how he had got into such a mess. Would they interrogate them? Torture them? Shoot them? About ten minutes passed and then another, higher-ranking, officer joined them and wanted to know what they were doing. He checked their ID cards and then instructed another soldier to take them somewhere. They were marched across the road and the grass verge towards the city centre. The soldier cocked his machine gun and for a moment Chris thought that he was about to die. Later, he found out that John and Paul had been thinking exactly the same thing.

Nothing happened and they continued their walk to a police station in the city centre. Inside, they were told to sit down on a bench in the lobby entrance. They sat there for a good forty-five minutes until they were called into the interior of the station. There, they sat in a ransacked office in front of a high ranking Iraqi officer who, through an interpreter, asked them what their jobs were and why they had been driving around. They all said they worked at the Messilah

Beach Hotel and had been out trying to buy basic provisions for their families. After a few moments, the officer said that they would have to travel to Baghdad with him that night.

"That's it, we're hostages," Chris thought. They managed to convince the officer to allow John to go across the road to a hotel so that he could telephone Sarah and tell her what was happening. But when John returned he had the Arabic hotel manager with him, who had not allowed him to call, but who informed the officer that they did indeed work at the Messilah Beach Hotel and should be allowed to return. The officer said he would speak to his superior and find out if this was possible. He left for fifteen minutes but returned saying that they would indeed have to travel to Baghdad that night. Almost immediately, they were marched across the road towards the Sheraton Hotel. Inside the lobby, everything appeared relatively normal, although it was obvious that the Iraqis had made a makeshift headquarters there. The men were ushered into the hotel ballroom where at least another twenty Westerners were sitting at tables, surrounded by Iraqi soldiers. They recognised some of the others and began swapping stories of their capture. Some of the people had been staying as guests at the Sheraton and were only in Kuwait on business trips. The whole group was comprised of men; there were no women or children. After two or three hours, they were all ushered to a Kuwait public transport bus for what was to be the beginning of the worst bus journey of their lives. The capacity of the bus was forty-four, so they only took up half the seats. They all tried to sit together near the rear but were told to spread around by the three Iraqi armed soldiers who had also boarded. Eventually, the bus departed. Nobody knew where it was going. They exited the city limits of Kuwait and began heading along the road to Basra. Conditions were pretty horrendous as there was no air-conditioning and the driver was obviously not well versed in bus driving; he seemed to think that he should drive the bus at full throttle whilst swaying from side to side. After an hour and a half, the bus suddenly left the road and began heading off into the desert along a track. Everyone thought that they would be shot, but after a while the bus stopped at a military camp and they were ordered off and lined up against the bus as soldiers walked up and down inspecting their captives. The driver and soldiers seemed to find the hostages' predicament very amusing.

Again, they were told to board the bus and it headed off. After several hours, dawn began to break and they saw Basra in the distance. They passed through the Iraqi border very quickly and, just as they all thought that they were being taken to Basra, the bus diverted onto a ring route. Everyone was disappointed, as they had been somewhat relieved at the thought of heading to Basra.

By now, no one had had anything to eat or drink for hours and the bus was stifling. A lot of the time people just sat alone with their thoughts, wondering how the hell they had got into this situation. It was particularly difficult for the guys who had only come into Kuwait on business and had been unlucky enough to stay at the Sheraton.

After what seemed like an eternity, they arrived at what could best be described as a desert burial ground. Looking out at the mounds as the driver slowed down was extremely disconcerting; they all felt they had reached the end this time. But the bus continued slowly until arriving at what looked like a military barracks, where the passengers were offloaded onto the sand. An officer appeared and told them to sit on the ground, and then instructed other soldiers to collect the contents of their pockets and bags. Chris, John and Paul had very little. After the collection, everyone was marched past a long line of prison cells housing several hundred Iranian POWs who must have been there since the Iran/Iraq war. Seeing white men, many of them assumed they were from the UN and asked through the bars if their families could be contacted and told they were still alive. They were obviously unaware that Iraq had invaded Kuwait. Everyone from the bus was put into a cell which was around fifteen by five metres. There were no beds, furniture or glass in the windows; just a stone floor and bars on the window openings. The door was locked and they were left to contemplate the last twelve hours. Disbelief was the general consensus. After a while, people started getting themselves into groups to discuss the situation. No one was prepared for it. People lapsed in and out of sleep, thinking about their families and what they must be imagining. Everyone was suffering from thirst, heat exhaustion and disorientation. Chris began thinking about the hundreds of other innocent prisoners around the world. He was afraid that, because of their remote location, they could be there for years, with nobody's knowledge. Eventually, a large dish of rice and eggplant was pushed under the door and a water butt was positioned outside the window bars. They did their best to cup their hands and drink the water. It was obviously polluted, but they were so thirsty they had to drink it. Then they ate, not realising that this would be the start of horrendous stomach problems. They spent one day in that hell-hole, sleeping on the stone floor with the rats and cockroaches while everybody started to get sick or have diarrhoea. It was awful.

On the second day, one of the officers came to the cell and began calling out names. Chris was the first called, and the solider beckoned him over. Chris was terrified, but he had the presence of mind to walk slowly in the hope that the soldier would also call out someone else's name before he reached him. He did. After a while, it became apparent that he was separating the British from everyone else. There were around eight Britons, who were led from the cell, through the camp and onto another bus.

This time, the bus windows had been covered with blankets and the passengers could not see out, except for occasional glimpses. The bus seemed to zoom around all over the place with no clear destination, stopping at at least three military camps of various descriptions. By now, the hostages were beyond caring about what they might do. They were just too exhausted and the seats of the bus were more comfortable than the floor in the prison cell, so many of them slept.

Incredibly, after several hours and many stops, they pulled up outside the Sheraton Hotel in Basra. They dismounted and were shown to the reception where room keys were distributed. The soldiers told them to shower and then come down for a meal. They were to spend the night at the hotel and the next day they would be taken to Baghdad from where they could travel to the country of their choice. "Bizarre" was not a strong enough adjective to describe the absurdity of the situation! They went to their rooms and, after cleaning their filthy bodies and using proper toilets, dined in the hotel restaurant. Having clarified with the secret police guarding them that they could drink beer, they proceeded to drink as much as they could in an attempt to dull the memory of the previous few days. Several Western military personnel wearing UN armbands were also dining in the hotel. Chris and the others made several attempts to pass them their names and nationalities in the hope that they would contact their embassies but they would not even acknowledge them. They did manage to get into the hotel business centre and phone the British Embassy in Baghdad to give them their names. Incredibly, the Embassy would only agree to note them if they could give them their passport numbers. Needless to say, no one knew the numbers and they had no idea where their passports were.

After one night in the Sheraton, they were woken early by guards and told to go to the lobby. Once assembled, they were put on yet another bus to begin another nightmare twelve hour journey, to Baghdad. Again, there was no water or food and there were blankets covering the windows. Eventually they arrived at the Mansour Melia Hotel, much to their amazement, and were once again allocated rooms. They spent another restless night wondering what the next day would bring. Early the next day, they were woken, told to go down for breakfast and shown into a huge function room.

To Chris' absolute astonishment, there I was, sitting at a table with other people he knew from the hotel back in Kuwait.

*

Still cuddling on the bed, Chris and I were shocked by the events of the past week. The tremendous guilt I felt about Sarah and the girls would not go away.

We stayed in the room until there was a loud knock on the door, announcing that it was time for lunch. Everyone lined up in the corridor of the eighth floor, awaiting instructions. It was a long corridor, partitioned in the centre by lifts, with rooms on either side. Outside the lifts there was a table at which armed guards sat, blocking any attempt to escape. There were usually six to eight armed Iraqi guards in civilian clothes, playing cards or listening to the radio and observing us, their handguns visible on the table. We were allocated a specific lift to enter and were accompanied by an armed guard down to the banqueting room. Once inside, we were free to help ourselves to food and non-alcoholic drinks. We could sit with whomever we wanted and listen to everyone's stories; we could even sit with the military men, who would periodically disappear. Hotel staff came around to the tables offering cigarettes for free; a mixture of Rothmans, Marlboro and the local Arabic cigarettes that tasted like camel dung.

We were given an hour or so, and then taken back to our rooms until the call for supper, which was a mixture of Arabic mezza, salad and lots of bread. We would only see John at meal times, as he was on another hotel floor. Chris and I were lucky; at least we had each other. The first night, we lay together talking about the dreams we wished to fulfil, if we were fortunate enough to leave Baghdad intact. We had *Baghdad FM* on some sort of central system coming through the speakers in the room. I cried and Chris held me as he tried to reassure me.

It was a great relief to be able to have a bath, but there were no toothbrushes or toothpaste, so my mouth felt disgusting. Chris and I were convinced that the rooms must be bugged, so we talked in whispers well into the night, which was when the paranoia set in. We did eventually fall asleep in each other's arms, drifting in and out of consciousness and listening to the noises of the city of Baghdad as life carried on as normal; taxis hooted their horns, people shouted. The bright lights of Baghdad were visible all around as I prayed there would be a peaceful solution to the situation.

<u>Wednesday 8th August.</u>

There was a loud bang at the door; it was time for breakfast. We quickly got up in the same old smelly clothes, washed our faces with water and joined the group in the corridor. It was the same ritual as the day before; going in the lift accompanied by the armed guards to the banqueting room, where Chris and I sat with John and Ian. As stressed as we all were, we tried to laugh and joke as much as possible, in an attempt to relieve the strain we were all feeling. John and Ian were housed on a separate floor to Chris and me, so mealtimes offered us the only opportunity to be together. The guards grew nervous if the hostages tried to gather into larger groups, and we quickly learned that this was to be avoided. There were more forms to complete, giving our names and the details of the companies we worked for in Kuwait and whether they were civil or military. We were now allowed visits by the British Embassy staff during specific allocated times arranged by our keepers. An Embassy official came once, with even more forms to fill in with our family names, parents' names, addresses and next of kin. Unfortunately, she was unable to tell us anything we didn't already know.

"I'll be able to contact your families to let them know that you are alive and in Iraq," she offered, before leaving.

During the day, we were allowed access to the hotel pool in groups, with armed guards to keep us company. For about an hour, we could sit on a sun chair or swim before being taken back to the room following the same ritual, with armed guards escorting us everywhere. On our way back, we had to walk past paying guests, who looked at us in disbelief, wondering what was going on. The Iraqi guards seemed friendly enough but they were nervous about the attention we got; they were a little unsure of the situation themselves. On this particular day, they had some treats in store for us. The British expats in Iraq had sent black bags full of items for us to choose from. As always, regardless of the situation, some people tried to organise, to be in charge. The clothes bags were sorted into piles, male and female. The clothes included underwear, trousers, shirts, shorts, t-shirts as well as books and board games like Trivial Pursuit and cards, Scrabble, pens and paper. We were very grateful for everything. The best bag had soap, talcum powder and toothbrushes, but—still—no antiperspirant. Tampons were still a problem as the expats had panicked and exhausted the supply in Baghdad. Although the women did manage to get our hands on some, we decided it was kinder to give the supply to a lady who was bleeding heavily and had been planning to go home for surgery. We kept the sanitary towels—or "nappies", as I call them—for ourselves. There weren't many, but we were thankful. I managed to get hold of a few t-shirts and longish shorts and tracksuit bottoms. As I was a trained nurse, I was allocated the first aid box, which would remain in my room until someone needed it. We even managed to set up a room with the books in it, like a library. By now, the guards had become more relaxed with us and allowed us to sit in the corridors to play board games and chat. We had access to local newspapers—all censored—which relayed limited information about the political situation. We had become a little complacent and found ourselves running on auto pilot. We were all just like robots, programmed to do as we were told. At times, we became depressed and frustrated. Some men, especially, were very concerned about their families, their jobs and what their financial situation would be after the war, and tended to react with emotional outbursts. One tried to commit suicide by jumping off an eighth floor balcony but, luckily, was prevented in time.

Although we were allowed to sit by the pool in the glorious sun for an hour or so every day, it really didn't help. Saddam took advantage of the situation for propaganda purposes and sent film coverage of his "guests" staying in hotels, enjoying his hospitality. When the British public saw the images, it looked as though we were all in a luxury holiday camp, which was far from the truth!

*

Morale was becoming low, so a little pampering went a long way. I cut Chris' hair, and Ian asked me to do his. I'm not a hairdresser, but it made us laugh to find ourselves sitting on the balcony with a queue of people waiting for haircuts! I told John that Sarah would kill me if she saw the bad haircut I'd given him. At least it helped pass the time. Through the interpreter, John had managed to arrange for contact to be made with the Messilah Beach Hotel in Kuwait so that he could receive news about his family. At last, he was told that they were still at the hotel in Kuwait and that all was well. They were free to walk about the hotel and were well looked after. Knowing Sarah, I suspected that she was probably in command! The men tried to persuade the guards to give us some beer. They eventually agreed and we offered to pay in Sterling with some of the money I had retrieved from Kuwait. Unfortunately, this was short lived. The beer affected the men in different ways. Some became agitated, arranging escape plans with a level of confidence that was dangerous for all of us. This made the guards nervous, so inevitably the alcohol stopped coming.

*

One day, while we were being escorted to the pool, Chris proposed.

"If we ever get out of here, let's get married!" he said. What could I do but agree? This glimmer of light in the darkness cheered us all up, including some of the men to whom we had become close, not to mention John and Ian.

In the rooms or corridors, we all relayed to each other the stories we had heard. Some were even amusing. One man told us of the armed soldiers in Kuwait who had surrounded him. One asked him to lock his car, gave him the keys and then handed him a receipt, saying it would be returned later. This story had us in fits of hysterical laughter; Chris said that the car was surely on the road to Baghdad with someone driving around in it as we spoke. The military men had a short-wave radio, so we all sat huddled together in the corridor, trying to listen to the BBC *World Service News*, which depressed us even more. Chris and I often sat in our room and listened to *Baghdad FM*. One song they seemed to repeat was Elton John's 'Sacrifice'. It made me cry every time I heard it, as it reminded me of our bizarre situation.

Thursday 16th August 1990.

By now, we had been at the Mansour Melia Hotel for ten days, while the Americans were in another hotel in Baghdad. Most of us still suffered from periodic bouts of diarrhoea, which we had come to accept as part of the situation; The Baghdad Diet; guaranteed to make you lose weight!

On the eleventh afternoon, we were told to pack our belongings into our black bags. By now we had basic toiletries and clothes, provided by the British community of Baghdad. I still had the medical kit. We waited until night, wondering where we were going this time. Once it was dark, we were taken through the ritual of going down in the lifts escorted by the armed guards and then split into groups. Ian was not with us this time as we were once again told to get onto the bus, curtains drawn as before, and nor was John. We would not see them for a very long time, and Chris and I would wonder many times in the months that followed where they were and what had happened to them.

It was midnight when we left, and we were driven through Baghdad for about forty-five minutes. Among a group were two little children: a boy of seven and a girl of nine. They had been on their way to Malaysia with their parents on the British Airways flight that had landed for refuelling in Kuwait. For their sake, we all tried to make light of the situation, but they burst into tears frequently. They could see how frightened all the adults around them were, and I could only imagine how frightened they must have been. How on earth could their parents explain why they were on buses with windows shrouded in blankets, surrounded by soldiers?

After driving along a dirt track, we arrived at what looked like houses in the middle of a desert, all surrounded with tall barbed wire fences with sheeting covering the wire fence. The bus stopped.

The houses were on two levels and there were four or more of them in a row. Through the darkness, we could see a huge building in the distance, apparently some sort of military premises. We were asked to vacate the bus and follow the armed guards into the central house. As we all walked through, we were profoundly shocked to see thirty beds arranged in an L shape in one room, all with blankets and pillows—there were thirty of us altogether. *What on earth were they planning now?* There was a lot of activity among the guards; raised voices, and total confusion.

"You'll be staying here now," we were told abruptly. We all put our black bags on various beds and followed the armed guards into another room, where they were coming in and out of the buses with hot Arabic food, drinks, watermelon and grapes. We had a toilet downstairs and another two upstairs—just great for people suffering from diarrhoea, even though by now people were past caring and embarrassment was no longer an issue. Apparently, the houses were new military officers' houses that were not quite finished. We talked amongst ourselves for a while and then decided to get into the beds. Chris and I went into one single bed, whispering under the blankets, predicting what we thought they were going to do. We held each other tightly and eventually drifted off to sleep, all thirty of us in the same room. The children wept and it was heartbreaking to listen to their parents trying to comfort them in the darkness. We really believed that the Iraqis were going to gas us all once the lights went off and the door was closed. I prayed that they wouldn't, or if they did, that we would all be asleep.

Later, we learned that we were in one of the Al-Taji armaments factories, north of Baghdad.

Friday 17th August 1990.

With great relief, we all awoke to lots of commotion the next morning. Once again, the guards provided a breakfast of tea and fresh Arabic bread. They came in with all sorts of supplies, even Arabic Sumer cigarettes. We were allowed to go outside and observe our new abode in the daylight. The surroundings were a little daunting. There was a tall fence covered in barbed wire, with some of the makeshift sheeting falling away from it. They had put up iron gates to lock us in. These were also covered in sheeting. Another two houses were also being prepared for us.

We decided to sit in the sunshine, so the men put chairs and sofas outside for us to sit on. The buildings themselves were built in a row of four or five in a small compound. From what we could see through the gaps in the tarpaulin covering the fences, we seemed to be in the middle of nowhere, although we could discern a factory of some description about two kilometres away. We could only assume it to be some sort of military installation. Why else would we be here? Chris reckoned we were around forty kilometres north of Baghdad.

Time passed.

The days were boring, and tempers were beginning to flare. The worst was going to sleep all together in one room, trying to make light of an increasingly trying situation. Chris and I stayed outside talking in the darkness, just to have some time without anyone else, apart from the armed guards nearby.

It wasn't long before the guards realised that the cramped claustrophobic environment was going to lead to major problems. People were becoming difficult and fractious and a solution was needed.

Soon.

Sunday 19th August 1990.

Late into the night, the guards informed us that we would be moving to a more comfortable abode. At one in the morning, they told us to pack our bags. We were still unsure about what would happen, so we just followed orders. Outside there were two buses with their curtains drawn as usual. The windscreen was also covered with a sheet, with just enough visibility for the driver.

The journey was quiet, except for the sobs of the children. We were all confused and a little numb, with no idea of what was really going on. Two armed guards sat at the front while we were driven through Baghdad once again, then onto rough terrain. We drove around for about fifty minutes. Eventually we stopped and were quickly ushered off the bus to a building like a prison; one storey surrounded by a huge barbed wire fence. The windows were covered with corrugated iron, which was a total shock for everyone.

We were at ar-Ramadi munitions factory, a hundred and twenty kilometres west of Baghdad. The soldiers told us to move quickly through the gate into the building. Once inside, the bright neon strip lights were blinding and the corrugated iron blocked out any natural daylight. It would not take long for us all to develop blinding headaches.

We were shown into a large room with sofas, chairs and tables. Outside, there was a long corridor with rooms on either side. There was a kitchen at the bottom, a toilet with a shower and two Arabic toilets—holes in the ground—for us all.

We were told that we would be shown to our rooms, married couples and families first. Chris and I were still panicking that they would discover we were not married as we waited for instructions. Eventually, we were shown into a room along the corridor, lit up like Blackpool with bright strip lights. There were two old, metal single beds with clean sheets and pillows. It seemed that a military office had hurriedly been turned into sleeping accommodation. With the lights off, it was pitch black because of the corrugated iron covering the windows.

Chris threw his black bag on the bed, and we both sat huddled together in disbelief. We all still had diarrhoea, so once again I had to go to the toilet. I asked Chris to come with me.

Arabic toilets are hard to use at the best of times, but when one has diarrhoea and has to shower afterwards they are even worse. At least we were all in the same situation and respected each other as best we could in such a bizarre situation.

Eventually, Chris and I fell asleep with the strip lights turned off and the light from the corridor shining through the gap under the door. As I drifted to sleep, I tried to reassure myself: Although the last few days had been harrowing, to say the least, we had not been harmed. We had been well looked-after and given food supplies and beds to sleep in. We didn't know the situation regarding food and water in Kuwait. I thought about Sarah and prayed that she and the girls were okay. I wondered where Ian and John were and hoped that they were safe. Most people in Kuwait would be too scared to leave their homes. We were all enclosed in a tin box but—so far—we were protected in Iraq.

Monday 20th August 1990.

We woke to an unbearable din of drilling and banging outside. Chris and I ventured into the corridor, still wearing the clothes we had slept in. Everyone had gathered in the main room; apparently the guards had arrived with eggs, bread, tea and water and tins of powdered milk. People tried to organise some sort of rota system with regards to food and using the one shower, suggesting different schedules for women and men.

Daylight was visible through a few slits in the corrugated iron fencing, but the harsh artificial lights were giving some people migraines. As well as the small children, our group included a mother with a teenage son, and they were suffering, too. Not being allowed outside—armed guards manned the entrance—was causing stress, as we were not getting any fresh air or sunlight.

Finally, we managed to amuse ourselves somewhat. We had reached a degree of acceptance of our situation, and everyone pitched in to try and keep the children entertained. The guards arrived with a television, video, more clothes and some pot plants. They brought paper and drawing material for the children—after all, they were fathers too, and they must have realised how difficult things were for them. The ladies were given dishdashers—Arab traditional dress—and we decided we would draw arrows on them so that they would be like real prisoners' clothes. Maybe we would wear them home, and arrive in Heathrow with them on! You have to have hope. Someone suggested we should do a few exercises, just ten minutes a day, to stimulate mind and body.

All the while, I kept thinking about my family and how distraught they must be, unaware we were relatively safe in military camps, but denied the freedom to go home. I sat outside in the darkness, listening to the BBC *World Service News*. According to the news, Egyptians had fled from Kuwait. Thirty of them had arrived alive at the Jordanian border in cargo containers with no ventilation. Kuwait was still in chaos, and any British citizens who did not follow the Iraqi government orders to congregate at hotels in Kuwait in order to be moved elsewhere would not have their safety guaranteed after the August 24th deadline.

The British government was telling its nationals to stay in their homes and maintain a low profile, but they had no idea what was really going on. Anyone who remained indoors was at risk from the Iraqi soldiers and other groups in Kuwait sympathetic to the cause. By the time I left Kuwait, things were already dreadful. People had turned into savages. There were young boys brandishing weapons; looting, raping, shooting. Before the invasion, European women had had to contend with harassment from men, but now it was unavoidable. With no one to control it, it must have been a living hell. As awful as the last while had been, I was glad I was not in Kuwait on my own. At least our situation was controlled to a certain degree.

<u>Tuesday 21st August 1990.</u>

We all had another restless night with the constant noise outside as the Iraqi men worked all night, trying to finish the corrugated iron and barbed wire courtyard. In the morning, we saw daylight for the first time in three claustrophobic days. The corrugated iron had been removed from the windows and was now surrounding the building. A six foot by ten foot area had been cleared for us to walk around outside with tables and chairs and a rope for a washing line. It was fantastic to go outside into the fresh air. It was a beautiful sunny day and the tops of palm trees were visible in the distance. We were allowed outside for fifteen minutes, and then escorted back inside.

The same day, a Mr Ahmed, from the Ministry of Industry, visited us in his green military uniform. He wanted to know if we required any urgent items. We asked lots of questions and he tried to answer them, but was unable to explain in any detail. We wanted to know what had happened to the other people from the Mansour Melia Hotel in Baghdad, but he couldn't tell us. Apparently his major concern at the moment was for our health. He even mentioned that he could arrange for us to have a short trip into the country to have dinner! Once again, things went from the sublime to the ridiculous.

Just let us go home, I urged him in silence. *I'm not really interested in these lies anymore.*

"Rest assured that you come first," Mr Ahmed told us. "You are guests of Iraq and although our country is in great need of food supplies, we will feed you before our own families!"

That was nice, but we were all innocent victims of the situation! Unfortunately for them, they would have to continue to feed us until the food supplies became very low, at which point we would also suffer.

*

At seven in the evening, an Iraqi General visited us, along with three advisors and an interpreter. They wanted to check our facilities. The general was not impressed with the barbed wire and corrugated iron fence. We all gathered in the main room and listened as he suggested that we might be more comfortable if we returned to the houses that we had vacated prior to moving here. Having moved five times in a very short period, not to mention the fact that we had adapted to the tin box with its mice and crickets, I was not keen to be moved again. We had a vote on the option of staying or moving and, thankfully, the majority voted to stay. But the General still discussed the possibility of moving elsewhere, so we had to wait and see. The BBC *World Service News* informed us that Margaret Thatcher was talking on our behalf, and not much else.

After the General, a doctor came to see us. He gave us some anti-inflammatory cream and tablets like Piriton to reduce the persistent scratching on our feet, hands and legs from the sand flies. Chris' feet were in a dreadful mess, full of open sores from all the scratching. At night, we wet towels and wrapped them around our legs and feet to try to stop the itching.

*

At night, when everyone else had gone to bed, Chris and I often sat up late and watched videos, which were always bloody, violent and warlike. Days were turning into night and vice versa. We had so much time to sit and think that the eagerness and hope we once cherished with regard to going home had diminished. I still clung to some hope, but what could we do but accept the bloody awful situation?

This night's video was "The Executioner", which seemed pretty apt! It was great to have the sitting room to ourselves, even if we had to wait until two in the morning. A good thing about staying up late was the possibility of sneaking into the kitchen to raid the fridge for a piece of bread and cheese without being scornfully observed by our elders. As we were still unable to eat vast amounts, it was difficult to eat at set times, and I am not programmed to eat when ordered!

People were starting to annoy one another badly. There were too many chiefs and not enough Indians. Of course, in these situations a routine makes things easier, but you can't enforce rules for adults. After all, we were all in the same boat, regardless of what positions we held on the outside. The power struggles had led to many minor conflicts, and now people tended to sit in their little groups. As usual, just a few of the men were the ones to upset the peace. It was interesting to note that the women were actually a lot stronger as time went on.

*

At first, the BBC *World Service* had been our lifeline to the outside world, but now it was becoming tedious; we were depressed to be reminded that we in our tin box were most definitely not a top priority as yet.

Two of the guards who had doubled as translators were transferred elsewhere. We now had two guards inside the building and more outside although, by now, they probably realised we had no immediate intention of escaping. Mr Ahmed from the Ministry of Industry still wanted to move us back to the original houses and despite our views we expected to move in a few days. We were all prepared, just in case.

Meanwhile, it was interesting to see how different people react to stressful situations. Some ate constantly, but I couldn't face food. I was upset about how little I could manage. The smokers among us were doing well getting through packets of Iraqi Sumer cigarettes, of which the guards had an endless supply.

Of course, we had the nice sunny climate of Iraq to be thankful for!

Then, the General came with the news that the men were going to be separated from the women and taken elsewhere. A guard began to call out men's names, asking them to move towards him in a line. The family with the teenage boy was told that he would go with his father, at which point the mother started to cry hysterically.

"He's only a boy!" she shouted. "Take me instead." We were all afraid that the men were being taken away to be shot dead and almost all of us were crying. The children clutched onto their parents, and we all begged the General to reconsider.

"I'm just following orders," he told us. "The woman and children will be going home." Then he left.

Later that evening, the General returned and told us that we could stay together, after all. We had no idea what made him change his mind.

Wednesday 22nd August 1990.

We awoke at one to the BBC *World Service News* after spending must of the night up and falling to sleep at around four in the morning. What was there to get up for, apart from listening to the BBC *World Service*, which was usually negative regarding our situation? Cleaners came in on a daily basis to clean the floors and give us clean bed linen. It was nice to have the opportunity to go outside in the sun amid the barbed wire and corrugated iron fencing for a couple of hours to pass the time. Chris was his usual kind self, reassuring me.

At meal times, portions were getting smaller, but there was still more than enough rice, meat and cucumber and tomato salad with lots of traditional Arabic bread. One of the girls discovered a black rat. We had already seen small brown field mice. The guards had supplied three old, rusty rat traps—Iraqi antiquities! Many of us still suffered from diarrhoea and the hygiene left a lot to be desired. The doctor had given us tablets for the diarrhoea, but the effects were always very short term.

The extra protein from mice droppings didn't help matters either!

Meanwhile, the BBC told us that leaders were still in discussion and that nationals from some European countries were going to be allowed to leave. These would be from countries that have had no military intervention, such as Spain, Italy and Ireland.

How I wished I had applied for an Irish passport, as I was entitled to do! If I had, I would have been free to go. Chris and I went outside, followed by armed guards, for a night stroll around the barbed wire and corrugated iron perimeter. We wanted to clear our heads; the disappointment of not being the ones to leave was becoming unbearable. The door was locked until the guards escorting us knocked to signal that we were ready to go back inside.

Thursday 23rd August 1990.

I was finding life in the tin box more difficult as time went on. The days passed so slowly. I prefer to be alone, so it was terribly difficult to sit in groups and talk absolute rubbish. On this particular day, I wasn't in the mood to be pleasant so I decided to meditate alone in my room. The strain was becoming almost unbearable. I couldn't breathe and suspected that I was slowly going crazy. It was like being in a goldfish bowl; swimming round and round with nowhere to go. This was definitely some form of mental torture! I pleaded with God that eventually we would be able to forget this dreadful ordeal and get on with our lives in a relatively normal way. But would it be so easy? Please God, our families were coping. I imagined that it must all be more difficult for them than me, as they had had no communication from me since the day of the invasion. I could imagine the horror stories printed by the media, and how they must be suffering. It was all very well for the outspoken politicians to voice their opinions about President Saddam Hussein, but when they were derogatory about him, they were jeopardising our position in Iraq and even our lives. Would they have been able to voice the same strong opinions sitting where we were?

"Negotiations will not be reached until American Forces move from Saudi Arabian soil," the BBC told us. This was cold comfort. We had been listening to the same news for three weeks now. Some in our group were the unfortunates on the British Airways Flight that had stopped for refuelling in Kuwait. Cath had been a transit passenger on her way back to Australia, and by now she had become a dear friend. She had adopted Chris and me.

"You remind me of my daughter," she had told me. "She's called Caroline, too."

Cath was really charismatic, and we often laughed with her. There was also another middle-aged couple who had been travelling to New Zealand on the same flight.

Chris and I still feared discovery that we were not yet married. We agreed that, if we had any problems, we would say that our marriage had taken place in Kuwait and that the legal documents remained there. As we learned that we would be moving once more, it was especially important that we not be separated.

Friday 24th August 1990.

By now, we had been in captivity for almost three weeks. Each day was more difficult than the one before. The night before, we had seen on Iraqi TV a televised interview of fellow hostages by Saddam Hussein. We knew the people concerned, as we had all been together at the Mansour Melia Hotel, Baghdad. Most of the interviewees were from the British Airways flight, and we had all stared at them on the screen in total disbelief. It was quite obvious that no one had the freedom to speak openly or to ask questions. They all looked frightened and demoralised. There was no sign of John and Ian.

Saddam Hussein also publicly announced that we would be allowed to send one letter each to our families. We were provided with pens and paper, so I started to write a painfully difficult letter to my family. To make things easier for them, I ended up telling a few white lies. I told them that all was well, up to a certain point, when all I wanted to do was pour my heart out and say how much I wanted to come home. None of us knew if we would ever see our families again, so many tear-stained letters were written, as we tried to be strong and told those dear to us not to worry. I knew that my wonderful parents would be praying for me and the others and could only hope that their prayers would be answered.

In the morning, we awoke to lots of noise and bare rooms. The guards had started removing furniture, kitchen items, fridges and food. As usual, a plan had been pre-arranged dictating who and what went where. We were all beginning to get a little irritated, including me, but I tended to let the spokesperson get on with it. However, the bossiness of self-appointed leaders was causing some unrest. We were all adults, after all, and did not appreciate being told where to go and having our accommodation allocated by another "guest". Hadn't we taken enough orders from our Iraqi "hosts"? One reason we had wanted to stay in the tin box was to prevent segregation and unrest, but now the tension was very real.

We were told to be ready to leave at nine in the evening, but at half past ten we were still waiting. Unfortunately, one of the fridges that had been removed contained one of the "guest's" insulin. The poor woman was an insulin dependant diabetic. She had supplies for two days, but she panicked, fearing that she would slip into a diabetic coma. The guards grew angry with each other and started screaming and shouting and the poor young woman grew more and more frantic. Fortunately, after a few hours the insulin was found.

After all the planning and upset over the allocation of accommodation, there was no guarantee that we would return to the same houses!

Most people sat on the floor in the main room to eat dinner as the furniture had gone, while the BBC stated that war was inevitable. If that was the case, it would be "khalas" to us, the innocent victims.

"Soviet patience is running out with the situation in the Gulf and it is more likely that they will deploy troops," the newsreader told us gravely. "Thousands of Egyptians have fled to Jordan. The Syrian border has been opened. Emergency flights are available to move Egyptians to Cairo. The Jordanian border has re-opened. More war planes have arrived in the Gulf from UK and USA. There has been great repulsion in the UK and USA over the televised coverage of Saddam with the hostages." It didn't sound as though anyone was doing much to get us out.

The radio also channelled some interesting tips from the Israelis regarding chemical warfare, especially about how to make your own gas mask. To do this, you need baking soda, water and rags. By immersing the rags in a solution of baking soda and water and wrapping them around the mouth and nose, you can combat fumes. A garbage bag is sufficient to protect the body. I was sure that this tip might be useful, but could only hope I would never need to use it!

*

Eventually we were escorted, carrying our belongings, through the corrugated iron and barbed wire fencing to a bus. The curtains were drawn and we were accompanied by armed guards. We sat silently, as we had many times before, waiting for the journey to end with no notion of what would happen next. We were, however, able to see through the driver's window as it had not been covered with a sheet. We travelled along narrow, winding roads, passing lots of palm trees and what appeared to be farms with donkeys and goats. There were many derelict buildings along the road side. The journey took between twenty and thirty minutes, bringing us to after eleven at night.

Saturday 25th August 1990.

After another dreadful night, we arrived at about midnight to find that all the items from the tin box had been set up in various places. We had all been allocated to the various houses. Little had changed other than the fact that all the windows from ground level had been securely sealed with metal covers. We assumed that this was to prevent us being viewed and vice versa. Try to imagine three houses surrounded by high wire fencing, covered in barbed wire with metal sheeting, and you will picture where we were. Around the perimeter of the fence, there were many military tents and armed soldiers, who looked like young boys. I managed to get some sleep and woke up at half past six. The air conditioning seemed to be making a dreadful noise, and a strange aroma seemed to be filling the room. In my confused state, I was convinced that we were being gassed.

Sunday 26th August 2005.

Chris and I spent the night sitting outside in the darkness with the light from the stars and moon shining on our abode. As we had become known as the house that never awoke before noon, we decided that we might as well stay up all night and cook breakfast at about eight. First, however, we would have to wait for the house that contained the food supplies to surface. We sat and talked and laughed throughout the night. Occasionally, we heard gunfire and the sound of packs of dogs and foxes howling in the distance. We were fortunate to have a constant supply of tea and coffee, and we were also able to cook some boiled eggs at four in the morning. The guards thought we were absolutely crazy to sit outside all night. We even put some chairs and a sofa outside the front door as it was so depressing to sit inside with all the downstairs windows covered with metal. At least outside we could look up at the night sky and gaze at the stars. We offered a cup of tea to one of the guards observing us. He was so grateful that we now had a new friend, who would keep us in cigarettes!

As the night came to an end, we watched the most beautiful sunrise while the other, more conservative "guests" slept. Luckily, the "guests" in the house containing the food supplies opened their doors at half past seven. Cath accompanied me to collect our provisions: eggs, tea, milk, tomatoes and bread. We had already consumed our rations during the night, much to the disapproval of the others. Chris cooked scrambled eggs, tomatoes and toast. The toast was made by turning on the electric ring and placing the bread on it, leaving a nice mess! We were all dreaming and salivating about pork sausages and bacon. Having said that, eating the feast in the yard was wonderful. After our fabulous early morning breakfast, Chris and I started to feel a little worse for wear. We went upstairs, fell asleep at about ten and awoke some time later to the noise of drilling. We had been allocated a room with a double bed all to ourselves, so things were looking up!

*

Suddenly, as we lay in bed, there was a knock on the door; the guards wanted to put up curtains and curtain rails. We were not feeling too good after only a couple of hours of sleep, so we stumbled downstairs for a cup of tea. The curtains were not finished when we went back to bed, so we were woken at two in the afternoon by another knock when the guards decided they were going to finish them. Once more, we went downstairs for another cup of tea, only to be informed that a TV crew was coming. I found it very hard to take this news in, having had such a disturbed sleep.

Our tea drinking was interrupted as an officer, Mr Adel, dressed in full military uniform and accompanied by some other soldiers, entered the room to hold a meeting with us.

"I want you to meet Iraqi ladies from the Iraqi Women's Federation," he informed us. "They'll be able to sort you out with women's things like toiletries, cosmetics, sanitary towels and tampons and so forth." We were touched, and the women we met were kind and spoke in perfect English as they compiled lists of our needs.

Then, we were told to make ourselves presentable as the TV crew would arrive shortly to film us all as a group.

"This is important," we were assured, "because it will ease the pain and suffering of your families." The film crew arrived at half past three to discuss the procedure prior to filming, and a woman photographer circulated among us taking our photographs to be sent to our families in the UK. The main instigator of this "circus" gave us strict guidelines about what we were allowed to say. We were told not to mention any political issues, but were free to show our feelings and comment on the visit of President Saddam Hussein with the other hostages. We were encouraged to praise Saddam for his kindness, and to make a plea for peace.

We reacted with complete disgust.

All we wanted was for our families to know that we were alive and relatively safe. I felt numb. The atmosphere in the room was horrible as a guard handed us each a piece of paper on which to write our names, home address and a message, which was to be vetted prior to our interviews. The pressure of pretending to be fine in such difficult circumstances highlighted the emotional weaknesses that so many of us had developed. Witnessing grown men break down and cry, while perfectly understandable, was terribly upsetting. But everyone was vulnerable, and some more so than others.

After the initial photographic session, individuals or couples were asked to take turns to sit on a sofa and relay their message. We all sat in the makeshift studio and watched one another. The main boss became increasingly agitated, as no one mentioned Saddam Hussein. He had expected us to thank him for his hospitality, but we all refused.

Finally, Chris and I had our turn. I started to shake as I realised how difficult it would be to relay a message and think about my family. Seeing the people before us break down had had a very emotional effect. I sat on the sofa and Chris sat on the armrest next to me. The blinding camera lights in my face were too much. As Chris started to speak, I saw an image of my family back home, watching the broadcast in horror. I felt my face twitch and my eyes well up with tears and I could not speak as I struggled not to break down in front of the cameras. They continued to film and Chris relayed a message for me, saying my name, and trying to lighten the mood: "Caroline still manages to put her make-up on!" The whole thing was far too traumatic for me and I simply sat on the sofa sobbing.

We were told that the interviews would be shown on Iraqi TV in a day or two. They had lots of editing to do and other hostages in different locations to film first. Eventually, though, the broadcast would be sent by satellite to the UK.

After that traumatic experience, we all sat in the yard drinking tea. We had often tried to get our hands on some alcohol, but our requests had always been denied. Dinner arrived at quarter to eight. The portions were smaller every day. This time, we had bread, fish and green beans. After the day we had had, most people wanted to keep themselves to themselves. An early night, it seemed, was just what the doctor had ordered.

Meanwhile, we were all suffering from the dreadful irritation and never-ending itch from the sand-fly and mosquito bites. We filled a bucket with salt water and passed it around, taking turns to soak our sore legs. This provided some temporary relief. Unfortunately, we only had one bucket, and sharing the water with everyone else's open sores probably only made things worse.

As we sat and soaked, we listened to the BBC *World Service News*. It informed us that the Austrian Ex-Secretary General of the UN had had an exchange of views with President Saddam Hussein, and Austrian nationals had been released. Lucky them! Prime Minister Margaret Thatcher, on the other hand, named Saddam Hussein as a tyrant and said that the UK would never weaken to such tactics. That was bad news for us.

And negotiations continued.

Monday 27th August 1990.

I woke up early. A dreadful mistake, as it just seemed to make the whole day drag on and on. We put the mattresses from our beds outside in the sun in the hope that this would kill off any bed bugs. By now, most of us were covered in terrible bites from the minute Iraqi sand-flies. We resembled dot-to-dot pictures with a mixture of small spots and larger, infected, festering ones. The doctor, a very pleasant man, was now visiting daily but all the lotions and potions he prescribed were ineffective and the persistent itching continued. Every day, we ritually had baths, using the infamous red bucket filled with salt water, to soak our limbs. The solution in the bucket was probably forming its own organisms by now! We all scratched our legs until they bled to try and stop the dreadful itch. Cath kept us entertained with her stories about the outback and the Aborigines, saying that her family would send her to live with them, if she ever returned home, because of our strange living habits in the camps!

The BBC *World Service News* reported that people were holding pro-Iraq demonstrations in London and that the Secretary General of the UN, Mr Perez de Cuella, would meet Saddam Hussein in Baghdad.

There was very little news regarding us.

One of the "guests" had become severely ill and we were especially worried about her because she was just a young girl of about thirteen. She had a fever of a hundred and four degrees and was vomiting. The doctor visited every four hours to monitor her condition, prescribing tepid baths and Paracetamol to try and lower her temperature. We all rallied around to help the distraught mother care for the girl.

Tuesday 28th August 1990.

When the doctor arrived at midnight, the invalid's condition had not improved so she was given an anti-emetic injection to stop the vomiting. She had not been able to keep anything down and she was starting to become delirious. The doctor wanted to take her to the hospital, but her mother was even more afraid at the prospect of losing her, and refused. At half past midnight, her temperature began to lower. We continued to monitor her throughout the night, sponging her with tepid water and forcing her to take fluids. A group of us sat outside until four in the morning, and Chris gathered some wood from around the camp to make a fire. It had two benefits; it was relaxing, and it helped to dispel the infuriating sand-flies. The guards laughed at us, thinking that we were crazy to light a fire in such humid conditions. We eventually went to sleep at about five, as our patient continued to improve. At half past two in the afternoon I arose to get a cup of tea and check on her to find that she had made a good recovery and was sitting outside. What a relief!

The BBC *World Service News* informed us that pro-Iraq demonstrations were banned in France, and would continue to be illegal until the hostages were released. An American in his fifties had died from a heart attack in Basra and would be flown back to the US after an autopsy. Finally, the British expressed some concern about British hostages, as there had been reports of some people with diabetes, hypertension and heart problems. Meanwhile, Iraq had declared Kuwait to be its nineteenth province.

Our response to the pro-Iraqi demonstrations in London was one of anger and disgust that such a demonstration should be permitted when we were unable to freely voice *our* opinions! It was a sad state of affairs, regardless of the fact that England is a democratic country. So far as we were concerned, certain legislation really should have been frozen until this bloody awful mess was resolved. If Margaret Thatcher, or somebody else of similar high standing, was taken hostage, would the British Government allow such fanatical demonstrations? I really didn't think so! It was like rubbing salt into an open wound. Perhaps the British would eventually learn from the French, who appeared to have a much more humane approach.

Later, the doctor bandaged my left foot. I had walked on the ground without wearing shoes, unaware of just how hot the ground temperature was, and had badly burned the sole. I had huge blisters and was unable to walk on my left foot, so the bandages provided much-needed support.

*

Food rations were diminishing. Milk and two cans of Pepsi were delivered; eggs were not available. It was great to have the Pepsi, which we shared. As our house was the "smoking house", Chris and I also received two packets of cigarettes and matches. We sat comfortably in the armchairs outside in the yard looking into the fire, drinking tea.

The doctor turned up again with a dilute hydrogen peroxide solution and some antibiotic cream for us to cleanse our sores with. Our constant scratching made everything worse. He also told us that Cath could go home. We all laughed, assuming he must be joking. But he wasn't.

"Why just Cath?" I asked.

He spoke so quickly it was hard to understand all the words: "At about eleven the news came on and Saddam Hussein publicly declared that women and children were free to leave Iraq if they wished, as of Wednesday." By this stage, everyone had gathered round. We were rather sceptical about this news as we had been lied to so many times before. There was a mixture of emotions; sadness and delight. There was also some bitterness as we realised that families would be separated, but all the men were adamant that the women should go. At twenty to twelve, we had a visit from Mr Adel from the Ministry of Industry, in his full uniform. He had heard also this latest news while driving, so he decided to see us in person to confirm it. We were still suspicious.

"No, really," he insisted, "the speech will be officially confirmed in the morning."

All along, we had hoped that we would eventually leave together as a group. That night, we sat around the fire discussing what to do. We decided to compile a list of everyone's names, addresses and contact numbers, just in case this was another ploy to separate us. I decided that I would stay with Chris.

"No, Caroline," he insisted again and again, "you should go!" But we had already been through so much together, and I still had very unpleasant memories of the time we were separated.

This was probably one of the hardest decisions I had ever had to make. I loved my family more than anything, but staying just seemed the right thing to do. Hopefully, we would return home together. I knew my family would understand my painful decision. I couldn't possibly leave, knowing how vulnerable the men would be, with no way of receiving information about their well-being.

I was also terrified that this was just another lie and that we would actually be taken to the desert, where we would be raped and killed. The Iraqis were free to do as they pleased. Who would know?

<u>Wednesday 29th August 1990.</u>

I had a very restless night, unable to sleep as my mind was doing overtime. I even asked Cath to wake us up early if there were any new developments. Why did they have to separate us all the time? At about one in the afternoon, Chris and I went downstairs and sat outside. I elevated my bandaged foot and drank tea. Nothing else happened until two, when the guards asked all those leaving to sign a piece of paper. They were told that they would be leaving at half past three, in the daylight. This made a change from travelling under the cover of night. There was slight nervousness, excitement and apprehension as people packed their black bin liners and distributed toiletries and other items among those staying behind.

The group that was to leave was composed of families with children and some middle aged ladies, including dear Cath, who had been a breath of fresh air. It was a terribly long wait for the bus to arrive and the atmosphere was very strained. One of the children in the next house was crying for her daddy to go too and this made everyone sad. We had become very close to these people—some more than others—and had accepted the most bizarre situations, so inevitably it was difficult to say good-bye. I hugged Cath and cried. Ever the joker, she invited us to visit her in Australia to attend the biggest party ever!

*

The bus duly arrived at half past three and we all gathered around. One little girl screamed for her father and clung to him tightly, not wanting to let him go. Her mother was also visibly distressed, and even the guards appeared touched. One wiped a tear from his eye. They were human after all, and had families, just like us. Some in our group were bitter towards certain nationalities, which only led to trouble. Regardless of our beliefs or political views, one thing I had already learned was that there is good and bad in all nationalities, and revenge will not solve problems.

Chris and I stood holding hands as we waved to the people on the bus, watching it go through the big iron gates. Then we sat in silence drinking tea and reflecting on events. There had been twenty-one of us, but now just ten remained.

We did learn that messages were getting through; apparently I had a message on the British Station Forces Radio from my family saying that they were all thinking of me. Unfortunately, I never heard it.

We were still sitting outside at half past eleven at night when a bus arrived. An American disembarked, carrying a large bag that contained tennis balls and two tennis rackets. He seemed to be deeply relieved to see Europeans. He had been a resident of Baghdad, free to come and go as he pleased until the day before, when he was picked up and sent on a long journey to reach us. Now, he joined us in the yard and we discussed the usual issues.

Thursday 30th August 1990.

The new American gentleman, Sam, was an early riser and he was busy introducing himself to the group when we got up. From the BBC *World Service News* we learned something of the fate of our former fellow "guests". They were back at the Mansour Melia hotel in Baghdad, waiting for exit visas and passports, and it was possible that they would get out on the first of September. European airlines had offered to supply planes to help with the operation, and a UN meeting had been postponed until the next day.

One of the guards came up to Chris and me at around two in the afternoon.

"Pack your belongings," he told us in broken English. "We're going to take you somewhere else."

It was far too early in the day for such a shock, so at first I really believed he was joking.

"What, just us two? Where are we going? Why?"

He didn't answer. Chris was in the shower when I yelled to him that we had to go. He shouted out of the window to one of the men and asked them if I was winding him up.

We had ten minutes to gather our belongings, which we put into our black plastic bin liner. I started to shake, not quite having a grip on the situation. Sam came upstairs with his address book. He asked me to write down my address so that whoever got out first could contact the others' relatives.

"I'm so sorry you have to go," he kept repeating. This made me even more nervous: *Does he know something we don't?* The uncertainty was compounded by the lack of communication. By quarter past two, we were outside saying good bye. I was crying and everyone else wore expressions of total bewilderment. Why were just two of us being taken away? I couldn't stop my imagination playing tricks. I could even picture the ritual that would undoubtedly occur once we had left; the others would all group together, make good strong tea and discuss what had happened.

Chris and I held hands as we sat in the middle row of the bus. As we left the buildings, the remaining "guests" all stood waving to us, just as we had done yesterday. The journey was like so many others, with curtains covering the windows. We went along some country roads, occasionally passing buildings. The guards sat and chatted at the front of the bus. We eventually got onto the road to Baghdad and saw a sign indicating that it was thirty kilometres away. For a split second, we thought perhaps they were taking us to the Mansour Melia Hotel in Baghdad, but after travelling for an hour, we suspected that we were not going there, after all. The guards appeared confused as to what direction to take and I was getting very scared. There were four armed guardsmen with just Chris and myself. I prayed we would arrive safely at our destination while the constant fear of rape made me a nervous wreck. After about an hour and forty minutes we came to a checkpoint where the guards had a short conversation with the soldiers who, after some discussions, allowed us entry. Three hundred yards from the checkpoint, the bus stopped and the guards got off. More guards arrived and then we were also asked to leave the bus, along with our belongings.

A large white building with very impressive brown domes, surrounded by greenery, trees and grass was directly in front of us. We had arrived at the Salman Pak chemical and biological installation on the Euphrates, south of Baghdad. We followed the guards along a short pathway to the entrance, where we were greeted by three Japanese men who were being moved now that we had arrived. We entered what had obviously been an office building not so long ago. There was evidence of filing cabinets, desks and a front office entrance area. We were ushered into a very spacious lounge, with a thick green piled carpet, Arabic sofas and chairs, two dining room tables and about twenty chairs. A television in the corner was showing James Bond's *Dr No*.

Chris and I looked at each other; this was a huge improvement! We sat down, placed our black bin liners on the floor and lit a cigarette. A young boy came in with some water and a man came and asked us about lunch. After a while, two official looking men appeared. The most senior introduced himself as he shook our hands.

"My name is Cassim," he told us, "and I will be your translator. You are our guests and we are here to make your stay as comfortable as possible, until you are free to go home to the UK."

Twenty minutes later, at half past four, four large trays of food arrived and were placed on the tables with water, plates and cutlery. I couldn't believe it; not only were people serving us food, but we also had a choice of menu! It was delicious, although our appetites were not huge after all the events of the past few days. After lunch, we were shown to our large, spacious room with four beds, a radio, water, shampoo, toothpaste, towels, two chairs and a filing cabinet for a wardrobe. There was even a magnetic three-in-one game of chess, chequers and backgammon. Unbelievable! In fact, after our last abode, it seemed luxurious. I was a little apprehensive about the four beds, assuming that others would eventually join us.

Our "hosts" arranged for a doctor to examine my foot, which was still bandaged. The blisters had become so painful I was unable to put any weight on it. The doctor removed the bandage and asked how I had managed to hurt the sole of my foot.

"It would hurt too much to lance it," he said as he cleaned it with antiseptic solution and re-bandaged it, "but if it's not better in two days I'll have to." I hobbled around our new surroundings, which were comfortable, apart from the toilet and shower.

Later, men started appearing, curious to meet the new "guests". We met two Japanese hostages who had also been in Kuwait; their wives and children had left the day before. There was also a man from Texas who had been on the British Airways flight.

That evening, we all sat down to the most delicious meal of hot food yet with trays of salads and meat. There was even soy sauce for our Japanese friends! The best part was two beautiful trays of fresh fruit with oranges, grapes and bananas. My face was glowing with delight. But by now we were not used to such nice goodies all at once. If we ate the lot we would pay for it later in the toilet. I managed to devour an orange, which was a real treat. In the main room there were also two fridges containing water, soft drinks, Arabic chocolate bars, oranges and grapes. After the meal, we sat in front of the television and watched an interview by an American journalist with President Saddam Hussein for a well known American news channel. It was entertaining, but no major issues were discussed and we were still no wiser regarding our own position. We continued to rely on the BBC, which told us that women and children were awaiting documentation before release, and on the *Baghdad Observer* which reported that all was quiet in Kuwait and that food and water supplies were good. "All Westerners are guests of President Saddam Hussein," the newspaper insisted, "not hostages, and they are staying with Iraqi families."

I was not quite sure which Iraqi family we are supposed to be staying with.

Friday 31st August 1990.

There was a loud bang at the door at half past twelve.

"Your food is here!" a guard shouted. We quickly jumped up wearing our clothes and joined the others. Chris and I had our usual cups of tea. It was another delightful sunny day in Iraq. I looked out of the window, uncovered by any metal or corrugated sheeting. The grass had been burned by the scorching heat of the sun. In one area, there was a table tennis table. Ever more extraordinary!

After three cups of tea, I decided to venture to the shower with Chris escorting me. The shower was a hastily put together afterthought, alongside two disgusting toilets that we shared with the guards, each lacking a lock. The shower and toilets had been divided by some wooden doors with the top areas open for the entire world to see. The toilets were frequently blocked with tissue paper and didn't work well because they were used so much. I held my nose; the stench was so revolting it made me retch, especially when diarrhoea floated around the toilet bowl, sometimes seeping onto the floor.

Chris brushed his teeth while I undressed in the shower, trying not to wet the bandage or my clothes. I quickly showered, endeavouring not to look at all the body hairs on the floor and walls. Dressing and undressing in the shower seemed the most sensible solution, as I did not want to attract any unwanted attention from our guards. I kept covered to avoid any confrontation.

For breakfast, I had an orange and tea and at about two in the afternoon we were allowed to go outside. We tried to play table tennis but my leg was still bandaged and painful so I sat instead. Cassim, the translator, seemed very kind.

"What do you want for lunch?" he asked, apparently concerned that we wouldn't eat. The truth was that our appetites were small. With the events of the last few weeks and the diarrhoea, everyone had been losing lots of weight. In fact, the larger people had been delighted. We had come to call it the "Baghdad Diet", guaranteed to make anyone thinner. Cassim asked us to write a list of our demands, and most asked jokingly for freedom and to return home.

More realistically, I asked for some fresh lemons to add flavour to the water, and a print or picture of Baghdad, to add to my collection in the near future. There was no harm in asking, so we hopefully requested beer. This request was always met with a smile of deep regret; apparently the Iraqis had received strict instructions not to supply alcohol to us. In previous camps, we stocked up on grapes and asked for yeast and grape juice to make some wine, telling the guards that the yeast was for bread making. We had always had a bucket half full of grapes waiting to ferment, just as we had brewed our own wine in Kuwait. Unfortunately, we had always been moved before we could sample the goods!

Later, I sat in the yard wearing tracksuit trousers and one of Chris' long-sleeved shirts, watching large ants removing small particles from the soil, transporting them backwards and forwards. It was hot. There were many new faces around, all masculine. The Iraqi soldiers in their green military uniform remained sitting around the entrance at a desk. Usually there were five or six of them, although sometimes there were as many as eight, along with the translators and tea boys. I was starting to feel pretty uncomfortable and always avoided any eye contact unless absolutely necessary. Cassim advised me not to wear shorts or any skimpy clothes. With so many Arab men around me, the only female, this could cause problems. Iraqi military were constantly arriving and departing. They chatted at the desk and looked at us with distaste. I rose and went to explore.

I discovered a washing machine in the back room, close to the kitchen. It was a very primitive one and I was not convinced that it would wash the clothes well, but it would be useful for undergarments, which I had been hand-washing in the shower.

*

Before supper, Cassim arrived with our goodies. As promised, he presented me with a coloured picture of the famous Iraqi copper works, showing an Iraqi man surrounded by beautiful coffee pots. Chris and the other men received a trendy pair of bright shorts each. Supper was fish, rice, salad and water. I was actually starting to feel hungry, having abstained from lunch.

After supper, Mr Akmed, a senior military officer, came and introduced himself. He asked if we were happy and if we required anything. He wanted to know if we had any complaints with the staff and if our accommodation was suitable. He told us that the doctor would be coming for medical check-ups and asked me if I required anything else for my foot. He shouted and ordered the guard to get a chair so that I could elevate it. This was more comfortable for listening to the BBC, which duly informed us that King Hussein of Jordan and Margaret Thatcher were meeting to talk about the Arab Peace Plan and that they disagreed strongly about withdrawal. Women hostages and their children would be leaving the following day on an Iraqi jet, while Iraq had been warned that it would have to both withdraw from Kuwait and pay penalties to it. It looked as though the world was getting ready for war: US forces were arriving daily in the Middle East, and Iraqis in the UK were not allowed to leave and had had all their money frozen. As the soldiers got ready, refugees from Iran and Iraq were going home. The Secretary General of the UN said he was optimistic, but he must have been the only one.

The news of an impending war left an awful, depressing chill in the air. What would happen to us if war started?

We sat up playing chequers with the two Japanese men until two in the morning. They had both been working in Kuwait prior to the invasion. We tried to talk; they constantly bowed their head and we returned the gesture. Their English was limited, but during the days to come, we tried to teach them some, while they tried to teach us Japanese. The fact we couldn't understand each other didn't matter, as we all had a common bond.

Saturday 1st September 1990.

Life went on. The women and children were still waiting to be transferred to Great Britain, Japan and the USA. I managed to eat some food at lunch time; falafel, an Arabic speciality made from chickpeas that I used to eat in Kuwait for breakfast. It didn't actually look very appetising, but I ate so as not to insult the guards. After eating, we were allowed to sit outside, with an armed guard within close range.

I found it almost impossible to sleep at night because of the dreadful itch from the bites on my legs, which were still covered. The humidity just added to the problem. Chris and I often lay huddled together, talking about our families and our dreams. I often cried to think that these dreams might never be realised. If we did die, my one regret would be that I never had any children. I lay sleepless, thinking about my family and what might happen to me. What would my family do about my personal matters?

The Japanese men were still discussing the chequers game from last night. Sezuki and Seguci said that it was a board game not seen in Japan. It was very funny to watch them concentrate in their desperation to understand the tactics, and even discuss certain play tactics in Japanese! Although everyone was concerned about their families, it was extraordinary how we had all adjusted to each other in this bizarre situation.

In the morning, the BBC informed us that Bush and Gorbachev were going to meet, while the Secretary General of the UN now stated that he was "disappointed" with the Iraqi foreign minister. Lots of Kuwaitis were still missing, and food and medical supplies were running out. Iraq continued to insist that Kuwait was its nineteenth province, while Margaret Thatcher said that the presence of hostages—us—in Iraq would do nothing to prevent an attack.

Sunday 2nd September 1990.

The bites on my legs were driving me crazy! The night before, I soaked towels in water and wrapped them around my legs to try and alleviate the itch. It only worked for a few minutes. The BBC had more news, telling us of as many as three hundred women hostages who had been released and had arrived in the UK. Negotiations with Iraq were in their second day, but the Secretary General of the UN was still "disappointed".

I listened to a service on the radio and quietly said my own prayers. Relaxing, sedate music filled the air. Maybe *too* sedate. Were these the right surroundings for listening to Handel's *Water Music*? My female anatomy had a lot of answer for, as I wasn't feeling good. I sat outside, reading and day-dreaming while Chris and Mr Sezuki played table tennis.

After the evening meal, a guard arrived with a pair of shorts for me from the local market. Not wanting to insult him, and touched by his kindness, I gratefully accepted them. Unfortunately, I was not really in a position to wear shorts.

*

The days and nights were becoming so long. Chris and Sezuki often played chequers well into the night while the television showed scenes of Iraq and its provinces as well as the usual propaganda images of Saddam's armies marching defiantly through Baghdad to music and songs declaring love for Saddam. We had been given permission to write to our families, which we did once again, making light of the situation in an attempt to avoid any further pain and anguish on their part.

Sunday 3rd September 1990.

War was drawing close. According to the BBC, Iraq had blocked its air space, and about three hundred senior military officials from Kuwait were in jail. There was concern about the treatment of prisoners, and ordinary Kuwaitis had protested by throwing stones and engaging in sniper fire. An Iraqi officer had been set on fire by protesters. Meanwhile, the Ambassador for Germany was in discussion with Iraq.

I eventually fell asleep at about five in the morning, as my mind was doing overtime again. I woke at seven with awful stomach cramps and tossed and turned until eight thirty. I decided to get up and use the shower before everyone else did, thinking that it would also help to ease my cramps. Before the shower, Chris and I went into the main room for a cup of tea, which was always left on the table in two flasks. As usual, Chris accompanied me when I went to wash. I closed the door of the toilet next to the shower, the one that was always overflowing with tissues and excrement, to stop anyone using it or looking over the top while I was showering. I quickly undressed, nervous that one of the guards might come in. After showering, I dressed as fast as I could, still wet. By now, there were ten armed guards, sitting at the security office that I had to pass each time I needed the shower or toilet. Many of the guards were not used to seeing European women, and generally had a low opinion of them, so it was always wise to cover up, even when sleeping.

The stomach cramps continued and I started to menstruate. I desperately needed tampons but, again, improvised with tissue. Luckily, a lady had arrived and was sitting with the guards. I tried to explain my needs to her in poor Arabic, pointing to my stomach. Thankfully, I still had a tampon left from before, so I showed it to her. She looked baffled, and then marched off to the doctor's room. I followed her. A guard was sitting there, so the lady explained the situation to him and held up the tampon for him to see. He was totally bewildered and embarrassed and suggested that we should wait for the doctor. I couldn't believe it. I wished I'd never said anything! I went back for another cup of tea.

Cassim arrived. He had obviously been told that I needed something from the doctor.

"Are you ill?" he asked. It seemed as though the whole male population of Iraq knew that I had my period! Twenty minutes later, Cassim arrived with a female doctor. I could barely comprehend what was going on; it would have been far simpler to have kept quiet. I explained the situation as best I could and told her that I was not ill. She finally decided that I must have a painful period.

"I'll get you some tampons from the pharmacy as soon as possible," she promised. What a relief—even if I just got a box of sanitary towels! I'd just have to wait and see. BJ, the American guy, was in hysterics. Although he didn't say anything about it, he was obviously aware of what was going on and was highly amused. I liked BJ, who was from Texas, although his family was originally from India. He was always concerned about his cholesterol levels. We sat and talked about India and about religious beliefs and how the poor are treated by the wealthy Indians. It made me wonder what had happened to all the Indian expats who had lived and worked in Kuwait. They often put up with the most dreadful abuse and cruelty and were separated from their families as they strove for a better life, working hard to send money back to India to support their loved ones and pay for their children's education. Unfortunately, they would return to much worse conditions than those they had known in Kuwait. The company I worked for had had many Indian workers; some highly qualified. They had all earned very little money. Abraham, who was a good friend, told me that when his salary was converted into Rupees it was far more than he could possibly have earned in India. I admired the sacrifices he made; waiting three years to see his family. Abraham was a Christian. The Christmas before, he had given me a Bible.

"You shouldn't have this here," he had said (Bibles are illegal in Kuwait), "but it will help you to read *Proverbs* in times of trouble, or when you miss your family."

Now, I sat outside and read the *Baghdad Observer*. The BBC *World Service* was becoming depressing. Today, it told us grimly that some women were still stranded in a hotel in Baghdad, and the latest advice for women and children in Kuwait was to form a convoy under the guidance of the British Embassy and go to Baghdad to get exit visas.

Tuesday 4th September 1990.

Another exciting day in Iraq! The BBC *World Service News* reported that the convoy of women and children—a hundred and forty eight women and a hundred and fifty five children—was travelling to Baghdad in seven buses. An Iraqi jumbo jet had brought two hundred Iraqis home from London. Meanwhile, international talks were ongoing. The Senior Secretary of the Arab Summit had resigned, and the Emir of Kuwait had said he wanted Iraq's withdrawal and the restoration of the Kuwaiti government.

The previous night, at around three in the morning, I spotted a gecko on the walls in the corridor. Chris tried to catch it as I squirmed in the corner. Fortunately, it was pretty small, but that doesn't help if you're scared of them! In his pursuit to remove it, Chris chopped off its tail, which then wriggled around on the floor. In truth, we should welcome them as they eat all the mosquitoes and don't carry diseases. Eventually, with the gecko gone, I made it to the toilet, only to find a huge cockroach crawling around the toilet bowl, with his many friends crawling around on the floor! I screamed and ran out. Chris told me to stop making so much noise and tried to kill them while I went into the other toilet which was full of faeces from the previous two days. It was too much. I started retching, and vomited in the sink.

During the afternoon, while we were watching Saddam's propaganda on TV, a small grey mouse ran across the floor. I jumped on the chair while the men tried to remove it. Shortly afterwards I discovered more geckos, this time in the toilet. By now, I was beginning to hide my fear. I can adapt to most situations, but it was difficult to overcome my phobia about cockroaches, mice, rats and geckos!

Chris played table tennis. In fact, our games had improved dramatically. The Japanese men loved to play, too, and it alleviated the boredom for a short while. Frogs, grey with white spots, jumped out of the hedge while I watched. We had often wondered about the noises coming from the hedge; it was a bit like being in a wildlife park. We had supper at about quarter to nine and sat up watching the television. As usual, *Love Boat* was on.

Wednesday 5th September 1990.

News came that our families were to receive special P.O. Box numbers in the UK, USA and Japan so that they could write to us. How exciting to think that soon we would know if they actually received our letters! Meanwhile, the BBC *World Service News* told us that King Hussein of Jordan warned of catastrophe in the Gulf if a diplomatic solution was not reached, and prayed that war was not imminent.

As I sat outside, I was approached by Mr Akmed. He was a big man in full green military uniform, with the usual moustache. Watching the other guards running around, patently less relaxed than before, it was very apparent that Mr Akmed had a very senior position. He appeared very stern, but was not unpleasant to me in any way. He shook my hand and sat down, speaking in Arabic through Cassim.

"Caroline," he said. "What are your views about the situation involving Iraq? How do you feel about being a guest here? And what is your opinion on the invasion of Kuwait by the Iraqis?"

I was in a very difficult position. What difference would my opinion make? I was just an ordinary person in the wrong place at the wrong time.

Trying to be diplomatic, I said that the European countries, along with Arabic countries, would have little respect for Iraq and President Saddam Hussein, as they had held innocent people against their will, including women and children.

"Wouldn't it have been better," I suggested hesitantly, "if a solution had been reached through discussions with Iraq's Arab neighbours?" As I said it, I realised that this was probably an impossible task. As long as the Emir of Kuwait continued to demand withdrawals from Kuwait and restoration of the government, absolutely nothing would be achieved. Mr Akmed listened patiently before offering his explanation: "What you need to understand is that that we do not *want* to hold you against your will. To save our country from military force, we have to use you for defensive purposes. Besides, it is unfair that so much wealth is distributed among certain families in Kuwait, when there is so much poverty and starvation in Iraq."

As I was taking this in, he continued: "Anyway, within two years or so, Iraq will employ Europeans to come to work, as they did before, in Kuwait as the nineteenth province of Iraq."

Of course, everyone has ideas about what is right and what is wrong. But who gave Iraqis the right to take everything that we had worked so hard for? All our personal possessions had been looted or destroyed and innocent Kuwaitis had been tortured and murdered.

Later, the female doctor, Cassim, Chris, the Japanese men and I sat while Mr Akmed asked us if we had any requests. In answer to the request for beer, he replied that we might get some in two or three days, *Inshallah* (God willing). He also mentioned President Saddam Hussein could call at any time to visit us. That explained all the strange happenings of the evening! Mr Akmed had been there for a long time, along with the doctor in her crisp white coat. At first, we didn't understand why they were there, but now it was clear that they were waiting for someone. They sat and joined us for the evening meal, which was a little strained. It was a bit like sitting with a headmaster and everybody was quiet.

Mr Akmed broke the silence: "Caroline, do you need any cosmetics?"

"No," I thanked him, "although they would be nice for when I go home."

"Of course, we do not know when you will be going home," he remarked with the clear implication that it might be a long time yet.

Now we understood the purpose of Mr Akmed's visit, as he asked us all about our views on the situation. He was testing the water to see if anyone held outspoken views, anxious to avoid any criticism. President Saddam Hussein would punish our keepers if we insulted him or were confrontational. Needless to say, some men were extremely angry and President Saddam Hussein never arrived.

A part of me was curious; what would it be like to meet the dictator? Was he truly a tyrant as Margaret Thatcher had said? Cassim had told us that when one meets Saddam, one is presented with a solid gold watch bearing his face. Apparently this was also his reward for soldiers who have shown great courage.

We asked Mr Akmed about other hostages in Iraq and whether it would be possible to send them a letter. He promised to deliver letters to John and Ian, who were being held far away.

*

That evening, President Saddam Hussein had a broadcast on television for the Arabic people with English subtitles. He asked the Arab Nations to join together and revolt against the aggressors; the USA and other forces.

"Iraq will not be defeated by Zionist forces," he said. "Who has the right to deprive children of milk? The Western forces would be responsible for deaths resulting from the inhumane action brought against Iraq."

Before turning in for the night, I read the *Baghdad Observer*, which posed the question: "Who is the war criminal?" and answered it by saying, "Thatcher is now fanning the flames of war against Iraq, by promoting a military settlement to the Gulf crisis. If such a thing happens, thousands of troops and civilians will be killed on both sides and the stability and security of the whole region will be in danger. It is Prime Minister Margaret Thatcher of Britain who should be hauled before an international war crimes tribunal."

It had been a long day!

Thursday 6th September 1990.

The *BBC World Service* News reported that Members of Parliament would return to discuss the Gulf crisis, while King Hussein of Jordan was in Baghdad. Cargo ships from Kuwait had left the Gulf, transporting Indian Nationals home. International bodies were providing help for refugees stranded on Jordanian border, with the International Red Cross providing food and medical supplies. Foreign Minister Mr Azzis was meeting in Iran. All medical supplies had been stopped in Kuwait, and any military force would have to receive confirmation from the United Nations. There was no consensus for war. The US Embassy in Kuwait had stated that an American citizen had been shot by Iraqi troops trying to avoid capture; the man was wounded and taken to hospital.

The main discussion of the day was about the plight of all the unfortunate refugees trapped at the Jordanian border. Mostly Indian and Bangladeshi, there were about a hundred thousand of them, living in the most appalling conditions in makeshift huts with mattresses everywhere. They were holding on to the few possessions they had. We listened to one Indian man's story as he spoke to a British journalist. The conditions were not fit for humans; the smell was horrendous, there were no toilets and people were simply lying on the sand, some with intravenous infusions of saline for severe dehydration. The United Nations had agreed with

Iraq that emergency supplies of food and medicine would be sent to these unfortunate people, who always appeared to end up at the bottom of the pile. There were reports of Jordanians selling bottles of water at extortionate prices, knowing that these desperate people would part with their only possessions for some water for their children. One cargo ship had left with about seven hundred and fifty Indian refugees on board, and the Indian government had asked other nations to provide help to take them from the borders to their homeland.

We felt both helpless and sympathetic as we listened to the stories of those poor people. I prayed that they would eventually be reunited with their families.

Friday September 7th 1990.

There was lots of activity in the morning as the guards prepared another room next door for some more "guests". Meanwhile, the radio informed us that Saudi Arabia was going to pay millions of dollars every month to cover the costs of the American forces in Saudi. Britain would be sending more military, America had begun to airlift its nationals stranded in Kuwait and the Emir of Kuwait had no objections to paying for the American forces. Altogether, there were a hundred thousand American forces in the Gulf. An emergency debate had been held in the House of Commons about sending additional forces to reinforce those already there. It had also been determined that United Nations sanctions against Iraq would have to be tightened—sanctions or war were the only ways to make Iraq withdraw from Kuwait. Two hundred and fifty women and children had arrived in London, and a Kuwaiti group calling themselves "Leaders of the Resistance Movement", appealed to the USA to help them as they were unable to defeat Iraq alone.

It was hard to take all this in, as I had had another disturbed night's sleep. The dreadful bites on my legs were turning to blisters that were swelling up like golf balls. I wanted to scratch and scratch, but that only made them bleed. At five in the morning I ran a cold shower on them to try and stop the itching, and again at half past five. This provided relief for a little while. Chris escorted me backwards and forwards to the shower room. Eventually I fell asleep with cold wet towels wrapped around my legs in an attempt to reduce the swelling. BJ gave me some anti histamine tablets, but these didn't help a lot.

*

All day long, the guards were awaiting the new arrivals, as were we. In the evening, the new "guests" arrived. We already knew one of them; Chris had played golf in Kuwait with Rob. The other man, Richard, was also British. They had been taken from Kuwait the day before, driven to Baghdad under armed military, taken to the Mansour Melia Hotel and transferred onto another bus to here. We all wanted to hear about Kuwait. They recounted that they had been taken from Ahmadi, an area to the south of Kuwait City. They had both been in hiding in Kuwait, confident they would survive as they had enough food and water to last for about six months. But things were difficult in Kuwait, and Arab nationals informed the Iraqi soldiers of Kuwaiti and British nationals in hiding. That was how Rob and Richard had been discovered.

They also told us about an incident in which three Indian men were caught looting a gold shop in the Souk area; they were shot dead in the middle of the street in full view in order to provide an example. Rob and Richard had spoken to an American man in Kuwait, who had been living with the American who had been shot, as reported on the BBC. They had both been in hiding, barricading themselves in their apartment with furniture blocking the doorway, as well as a door chain. An Iraqi soldier pushed open the door and was trying to remove the door chain, when the American closed the door on the soldier's arm. Angry, the soldier shot at the door, got into the apartment and shot the man in the hand. Still resisting, he tried to grab onto a rope hanging from the window but he fell and broke his leg, and was taken to hospital. His companion said he did not want to resist capture and would go to Baghdad with the soldiers, rather than get shot.

Many people were still in hiding in Kuwait. Some were hidden in bathrooms, and most had a radio and received information from the BBC *World Service News.* They were unsure whether to leave as requested. All over the city, shops and supermarkets were being looted by the Iraqi soldiers and the military bus the Americans had travelled on from Kuwait was full of stolen goods. Apparently, the exiled Kuwaiti Government would compensate for loss of contracts, homes and personal possessions.

After eating, Rob and Richard had a surprise for all of the dry-mouthed alcoholics; they had managed to get a small quantity of gin and Scotch. We all had a small glass of gin which we mixed with Pepsi. The Scotch was saved for later. We savoured the taste of gin, drinking it slowly. Real alcohol—a reason to celebrate!

There was a late news report at midnight saying that all Westerners in Kuwait must give themselves up, and that they would be put in hotels in Baghdad.

Since arriving in Kuwait, I had learned that the stereotype that expats drink a lot is often true. With many alcoholics about (even in dry states such as Kuwait, people just brewed their own, or diluted Ethanol or Flash), I had been warned by a female friend to be wary of the expat men, who usually fell into one of the "three D's"; Divorced, Drunk or in Debt!

Saturday 8th September 1990.

The BBC *World Service News* told us that diplomatic efforts to diffuse the situation continued, the refugees in Jordan continued to suffer and the price of crude oil had fallen sharply. Bush had arrived in Helsinki to discuss talks on the crisis with Gorbachev. There would be an Arab Summit meeting the following day and India had begun airlifting from Jordan.

Chris and I avoided breakfast and managed to surface just before lunch. I managed to eat an orange and drink some tea. Rob gave me a Gerald Seymore book to pass the time, although I was feeling lethargic. As usual, I had spent most of the night trying to alleviate the persistent itch, and the humidity simply added to the problem. At five in the morning, Chris had applied some medicated cream and rubbed dry salt on my legs before wrapping them in wet towels.

Cassim the translator sat with me. He was always apprehensive about discussing our situation or President Saddam Hussein. In fact, it was very apparent that all the Iraqis with whom we had regular contact were particularly careful not to make any derogatory comments, fearing severe punishment if overheard by the guards.

Every day, we received the *Baghdad Observer*, which was generally full of propaganda, covering Iraq and its plight against the tyrants of the West. Unfortunately, the truth about the outside world had never been disclosed to the people of Iraq, and the way the news was presented was a form of brainwashing. The front cover always showed a picture of Saddam Hussein.

*

There was always a lot going on. Cars arrived constantly and new faces, especially guards, came and went. Today, however, a lorry of armed soldiers drove past the outside gate. This was strange, as normally the soldiers within the boundary were the ones at the checkpoint at the main gate.

"Those are soldiers with disabilities," Cassim explained, "such as problems with their eyesight or general health." They were classified as unfit to join the forces at the front line, so they helped with farming the land locally.

More people were coming! The guards prepared a room with three beds. When we asked who it would be, we were told that it was a family. At around ten that night, the men were playing Scrabble and I was reading, tucked away in the corner of the room, when two men walked past, followed by a third. They were escorted by the armed guards to their room, after which they came into the main room to join us. Marc and Jon were French while the third was an English man, Jay. They all looked very frightened and bewildered and were obviously surprised to see me, the only female. The doctor arrived and examined the Englishman, Jay, who had a history of cardiac problems. He had been recovering from bypass surgery in Kuwait and was on medication but not feeling well. He was mainly—and unsurprisingly—suffering with shortness of breath. With his sallow, greyish complexion and gasping breath, he certainly did not look the picture of health! Jay, who was about sixty, was given oxygen with a portable oxygen tank, which eventually provided him with some relief. I hoped and prayed that he wouldn't die; not here, like this. He stayed in his room with the doctor while Marc and Jon joined us. They were more than relieved to discover that we were being pretty well treated in the bizarre circumstances. The only doubt I had about the situation was that we were now ten, of whom I was the only female. This would not really be an acceptable situation in the eyes of the Iraqis. I wondered if they would move us on again tomorrow. Personally, I didn't mind being the sole female, but I would have to wait and see.

Cassim mentioned to the doctor that I required antihistamine tablets for the constant itch on my legs. I was seen and examined by a junior doctor as well as the senior doctor, who gave me another tube of cream and more antihistamine tablets. I hoped that I would be able to sleep later.

Before we all turned in for the night, Jay came to join us. He was a real character, who had been taken from Kuwait by force on the second of September. The soldiers had become very violent and Jay had been manhandled and thrown on the floor. His shirt was torn and covered in blood as he resisted capture. Soldiers had beaten civilians with their rifles, and Jay told us about an Englishman who had resisted capture and whose wife had been kicked and beaten with a rifle. The Frenchmen relayed a similar story; Kuwait was not a safe place to be. We stayed up into the early hours, swapping stories of how we all ended up in Iraq. To everyone's delight, Rob brought out the Scotch. Jay wanted a cigarette, much to everyone's horror. After surviving bypass surgery, we didn't think he should risk it! We voiced our concern, to which he retorted as he sipped his Scotch, "I may die in this hellhole, so I shall make sure I enjoy it before I go!"

<u>Sunday 9th September 1990.</u>

The BBC *World Service News* informed us of a meeting in Helsinki between Gorbachev and Bush. American troops would remain in the Gulf until Bush felt safe with the situation. The Soviets were reluctant to become involved in military conflict, but everyone agreed that Iraqi aggression would not be tolerated. Iraq's withdrawal from Kuwait to resolve the crisis peacefully was demanded. Evacuation flights had left Iraq for Jordan and the US. The superpowers sent warnings to Baghdad, and also stressed the need for reaching a diplomatic solution.

Boredom was a major problem. People had started to isolate themselves and retreat to their rooms. The atmosphere was strained and tense, with more people and so many different nationalities.

The toilets were disgusting. One of them only worked if the water tank above the toilet bowl was filled after each flush; the guards didn't bother, resulting in one of the toilets being full of faeces all the time. The stench was stomach churning, so I always held my nose or threw up. With the nine men as "guests", and the seven or eight guards who also used the washroom facilities, hygiene was not a top priority! The shower was covered in pubic hair, which was also moulded into the soap, and the sinks were always left full of hairs from the guards trimming their moustaches.

While I sat reading in the room, I discovered a mouse running across the floor before it went out through the gap under the door. How many more could there be? I ran out to join the others to eat, and afterwards we were allowed to watch the English news, which was monitored and edited. It showed anti-war demonstrations outside the American Embassy in London. People were totally against military force in the Gulf.

After the news, *One Flew over the Cuckoo's Nest* with Jack Nicholson followed. It seemed very apt! We all joked about it, re-enacting certain scenes and relating them to how we would behave if and when we were released. The film stopped the boredom for a couple of hours before Chris and I decided to go back to our room at half past one, leaving the men talking and playing cards. I looked around for any sign of mice and then listened to Richard Baker's music on the BBC. Eventually I lay in the bed listening to Vivaldi's *Four Seasons*, always one of my favourites.

We knew that another "guest" would be arriving the next day, as the two Japanese men had been asked to pair up.

Monday 10th September 1990.

We were so fed up by now. The men were becoming irritable. We weren't even afraid any more, but just waited for news of our plight. Not knowing what would happen to us was torture. If there was a war while we were all still in captivity, what would happen to us?

Every day, we went outside to the yard area. Chris had attached fire sand buckets to a broom pole, one either side, to use as weights. He used material from a torn T-shirt to hold the sand buckets in place and prevent them falling off. The armed guards stood and watched in amazement, and eventually a couple of them joined in. I tried to exercise in the room—although the guards seemed OK, I felt better away from their prying eyes and distorted views of Western women—which wasn't easy with my bandaged legs, but even moving my arms about for fifteen minutes or so helped with the boredom.

It was interesting to compare the BBC news with that on *Baghdad FM*. The BBC told us that member countries of NATO would supply ground troops. There were more warships in the Gulf and conditions in Kuwait were deteriorating, leaving people without electricity.

Baghdad FM, on the other hand, said that President Saddam Hussein had offered free oil to the third world, Iran had an agreement with Iraq and had renewed diplomatic relations after ten years of war and that there were demonstrations in Baghdad outside the American Embassy, with about ten thousand people opposing the war in the Gulf.

The British Embassy had asked for British citizens in Kuwait or Iraq to leave, following the various evacuation procedures. Chris and I looked at one another, both having the same thought; should I leave?

"Maybe you should go," Chris suggested. "It's getting tenser here by the day." But neither of us liked the idea of me travelling alone with four or five guards towards an unknown destination, who knew how far away. It was unlikely that Chris would be allowed to travel with me, and I had a lingering fear that maybe I wouldn't reach my destination at all. I didn't want to risk being one of those people who just disappear; I felt safer with Chris. It was also possible that there could be further delays or that the Iraqis could stop any further evacuations. They appeared to change plans on a regular basis. What if I was left in Baghdad alone?

I decided to stay put.

Later in the morning, Jay was taken to a hospital in Baghdad to have X-rays and further tests. He was terrified: "Don't let them take me!" He gave me his family's address and telephone number, in case he never returned. There was a lot of concern for his health, especially with his history of cardiac problems. The General had made the decision, and together with the medical staff he would determine if Jay should remain in hospital.

We all waited anxiously for news about Jay. We were a little concerned about how he would react. Although he was a likeable rogue, he was also a cantankerous so-and-so, prone to dramatic outbursts. Thankfully, in the late evening Jay returned, telling us about his visit to the disgusting hospital. It was filthy and dirty with soiled beds and dreadful smells emanating from the toilets that had made him throw up. He refused to go into two of the toilets that were full of faeces, so eventually they found him one which *only* had urine all over the floor. The doctors discussed his condition but he refused to stay in the hospital. As he said, there was more chance of dying from disease in the hospital than in the camp. The people of Iraq had little chance of survival if that hospital was anything to go by! Jay decided that if he kept quiet and avoided further attention, perhaps he would be left alone. He had been on medication in Kuwait, but in the struggle with the armed soldiers, one of them threw his tablets all over the floor. He had been pulled off a couch and hit on the head with the soldier's rifle. His shirt had been torn and his hands were cut and bleeding after the scuffle. It was obvious that Jay was frail and unable to fend for himself, so what these young soldiers gained from terrorising him was hard to imagine. Their colleagues looted his apartment, throwing the video recorder across the room and breaking it, along with the furniture. Jay had told us about how the rest of the soldiers gathered in his apartment with the goods they had looted from the other apartments in the complex. They threw a box containing jewellery on the floor and started dividing the goods among themselves.

On his way to a bus outside the apartment block, Jay told an Iraqi officer what had just taken place, and he was taken back to his apartment to try and retrieve his medication from the floor. His place was a total mess. The furniture was broken and everything of any value missing, including his home brew.

Kuwait was certainly not as calm and organised as the picture portrayed on Baghdad television. Kuwaiti resistance groups were fighting the Iraqi soldiers after nightfall, shooting and setting vehicles alight. For fifty Kuwaiti Dinars, one could buy weapons, so young Arabs, including non-Kuwaitis, were buying guns and tanks and causing chaos as they carried out their Rambo acts.

To our delight, Chris managed to tune in to the new *GulfLink* programme that evening, which for just fifteen minutes allowed families back home to relay messages to their loved ones, caught up in the dreadful crisis in the Gulf. Minutes before it finished we heard a message for Chris, John and I from a friend who had been teaching in Kuwait but had managed to get out before the invasion. It brightened us up to know that people were still thinking about us. As she didn't mention Sarah, Chris and I assumed that she was now safe and in Egypt or the UK.

The same evening, we heard without surprise the "No Comment" from President Saddam Hussein regarding the Arab Summit meeting between Gorbachev and Bush. We saw his speech on Baghdad TV and listened as he offered free oil to Third World countries and managed to totally avoid the main issues.

Tuesday 11th September 1990.

Good morning Iraq! I thought with a groan as I awoke to sunshine and the usual flies and fleas.

*

I managed to eat some lunch, avoiding any of the meat dishes. One of the men had had a severe bout of diarrhoea the day before, after eating a meat dish that hadn't smelled very fresh, so now we were all vegetarian. I finished my book and started to read another, there being little else to do. The men played chequers, chess and Scrabble. Chris and I played Scrabble in our room and read. Time passed slowly.

I watched the men walk in circles around the building, as a form of exercise. BJ was concerned about possible delayed reactions to recent weeks. He wondered if we would have psychiatric problems. I hoped not. But we were beginning to suffer the effects. We usually looked forward to reading the *Baghdad Observer*, but now we lacked interest. It was always propaganda, so there was no point.

By now, I had really come to despise the guards. On this particular day, as I sat outside, some workers walked past, looking and sniggering. They seemed to be delighted that we were there against our will. It's that sort of thing that really makes one dislike people. The guards were obviously enjoying and taking advantage of the situation. Why there were so many of them was beyond me. One or two of them repulsed me; always looking at me and talking about me in Arabic. Chris was always anxious when they were guarding us.

Having given up on the *Baghdad Observer*, we relied on the BBC for news. Today it told us that Iraq would allow a British diplomat to visit Kuwait to help women and children. The Swiss Embassy was closing, because of people fighting for food outside it, and Turkey had confirmed that thirty to forty thousand troops would be sent to Iraq. Things were a little better for refugees, and a hundred and ten flights had left to bring Asians home.

Failing all else, a mouse provided excitement. It ran under the filing cabinet in the room, so I screamed and jumped on the bed. Chris ran in and eventually the mouse escaped through a gap under the door. But later, when I went to the bin, the mouse jumped out, much to my horror. Again I screamed and ran into the main room, to the men's astonishment. There was huge relief and laughter when they discovered it was caused by a mouse! Back in our room, Chris was sitting on the bed, pale with fright.

The mouse had disappeared once again.

That evening, Chris, Jay, Rob, Richard and I tuned in to the *Gulf Link* radio broadcast and waited for messages from our families. It was always very emotional, listening to requests from wives to their husbands. A message for Sarah from her mother-in-law told her to contact the Egyptian Embassy in Kuwait. Sarah and her children must still have been in Kuwait. I broke down, imagining the worst.

At ten that night, Jay came and told us that he was being taken to hospital in Baghdad. As usual, he had had no warning, but we were all used to being moved around. I hoped, for Jay's sake, that he would be another step closer to going home on medical grounds. We were all liabilities to the Iraqi government, but with his medical history Jay was a bigger risk. Poor Jay looked so bewildered as he was escorted outside by two guards.

Wednesday 12th September 1990.

The BBC *World Service News* told us that an Iranian religious leader wanted Muslim leaders to set up troops as a defence for Holy War. Syria was to send more troops to Saudi Arabia. Iraq would not allow food to be distributed to refugees unless it was in charge. Four hundred Western women and children from Kuwait had arrived in London, while Iraq was applying force to the Kuwaitis.

It was quiet in the camp. A few of us had severe diarrhoea—not very pleasant as we shared the toilet and had to spend twenty minutes trying to flush it! The stench from the toilet and shower room was horrific, and I did not feel well. I sat in our room, playing Scrabble with Chris for two hours. Later, Chris played Trivia in French with Jay and Marc, translating some questions into English. It took forever.

We continued to wait and hope. After the games, Chris and I had a walk around the yard area.

"When this is all over," Chris asked, "will we get married and settle down at home for a while? We can always think about going overseas again in a couple of years." We both yearned to live in a beautiful cottage in the country. The thought made us smile and gave us hope. Our families would be delighted to have us safe at home.

*

In the evening, I was not hungry but decided I should eat some bread. We stayed up talking to Mr Sezuki until five, and showered at half past five. Rather than going to bed, we waited up for the *Gulf Link* broadcast at quarter to nine. It was so quiet at night. In the kitchen, which was disgusting and dirty, there was a full rubbish bag in the corner. As a mouse jumped out, I screamed, and backed out of the kitchen straight into Marc and Jay, who both laughed. The men were becoming used to my screams, and were always relieved when the cause was just a mouse! I followed them into the kitchen, but the mouse had disappeared.

"What are you doing up so early?" Marc and Jay asked. As we sat down for tea, bread and cheese, they were even more surprised to discover that we had stayed up all night. The guards were still sleeping in the front security area.

We tuned in to the radio broadcast and were disappointed that there were no messages, especially as we had waited all night. At that, Chris and I decided to go to sleep for a few hours.

Thursday 13th September 1990.

After collapsing in bed, we awoke at five thirty in the afternoon to find Jay in the main room. He had been monitored in the Cardiac Unit, and they had been controlling his medication for the past few days. He looked shattered.

"I can't sleep," he told us, "and I'm not bloody well going to eat."

The hospital staff had been very concerned about his condition but he had asked to come back here, as it was very clear he would not be released to go home. The staff had changed his medication, and were observing him. Thankfully Jay was not as short of breath as he had been, because he had been given oxygen in the hospital, which had given some short-term relief. The hospital had been an improvement on the first one, but was still pretty primitive and Jay was clearly relieved to be back. We sat talking until five, unable to sleep. Would life ever be normal again? As our "day" drew to a close, we tuned in to the BBC from which we learned that Iraqi authorities were withholding food from foreign nationals and that Syria prepared to send more troops.

Friday 14th September 1990.

Marc banged at our door, making Chris and I jump; we had only had about two hours sleep. It was time for the *Gulf Link* broadcast. It was usually impossible to hear it clearly at night, but it was repeated in the mornings. The morning was now the most important part of the day, as there was just a glimmer of hope that we might receive a message. This time it was worth it. I received a message loud and clear from some friends of the family. I felt wonderfully elated, but Chris was upset that he still hadn't received a message. Everyone waited silently together; British, French and Japanese. This was our lifeline to the outside world.

Despite having had little sleep, Chris and I decided to stay up.

*

By now, my legs were improving. There were still lots of bite marks, but the itch was a lot better. Still, it was very humid, which made us drowsy and I often lay on the bed drifting in and out of sleep.

In the evening, ten plates were placed on the table. To our complete surprise, on each plate there was just one piece of what resembled chicken, some pickles and bread. We called the bread "stone bread" as it was so hard—almost inedible—and we could see weevils baked into it. Even the guards looked a little surprised. We assumed that this was supposed to prompt us to write home to say that sanctions were taking effect. The men were angry and refused to eat it. Presumably the eight guards had their own supply of food. There was no tea, either. As we left the table, the guards threw everything into the disgusting, smelly kitchen and most of us went to bed early, fed up with the whole situation.

Iraq was no longer headline news. On the BBC *World Service* there was a story about a massacre in the South African townships. I supposed we should be thankful for small mercies. The only news we received about Iraq was via Iraqi TV or Iraqi radio, which usually discussed bloodshed and unrest in the world, or demonstrations on Iraq's behalf with plenty of adoration for Saddam Hussein. Instead of adverts, Iraqi TV showed President Saddam in military uniform, clips of his past meetings with political figures and celebrations. One frequent rerun was of the military on the Persian Gulf shores in Kuwait, singing and smiling. Another was of Iraqi POWs returning home from the Iran-Iraq war, some of whom had been imprisoned for eight or nine years. They disembarked from the buses clutching pictures of President Saddam Hussein.

Saturday 15th September 1990.

It was difficult to wake up and, as a result, we missed the *Gulf Link* Broadcast, struggling out of bed at around noon.

By now, meals were being rationed. Soon we would all be suitable candidates for anorexia clinics! The Iraqis arrived with some type of pancake filled with a disgusting mixture and a dish of tomatoes and cucumber. We all avoided the pancakes and made do with some cheese from the fridge and a little "stone bread". Most of us had diarrhoea, as the standard of hygiene was a huge problem. We took care to avoid any food with filling or meat, especially today as two rather unclean ladies were preparing the food with visibly dirty fingernails.

The food was becoming more and more meagre. We decided to try and salvage things like fruit and small packets of biscuits to hide in our rooms to prevent the guards from stealing them. We had seen them taking bags of food that arrived, and giving us the leftovers. I could only assume that the food was for their families. One locked room was stocked with biscuits, cigarettes and other goodies, which they must have been storing for themselves and their families. It was understandable; most of them were poor. Why should we benefit? After all, we were the enemy and indirectly responsible so far as they were concerned for the sanctions imposed upon them.

Another British man arrived. He had been on business in Kuwait for two days but had unfortunately picked the wrong two days and ended up hiding in an Embassy apartment, until he was discovered by the Iraqi soldiers. He had been roughly treated and had stayed at the Al Mansour Melia before being transferred to our accommodation.

*

That night, at around midnight, there was lots of noise in the corridor. Chris opened the door to investigate and discovered that Jon had been told that he had received a telephone call to say he was to be driven to the Al Mansour Melia, after which he would be released to go home to France. Jon's expression revealed a turmoil of emotion; a mix of happiness and apprehension. He knew as well as the rest of us that he could not rely on what he was told. I shook his hand, gave him a hug and congratulated him on his imminent release. The still sleepy guards walked around in their traditional dishdashes, with the official uniformed officers who were to escort him. Communication between the guards and officers was practically non-existent and our guards obviously had no idea what was going on.

Before Jon left, Chris and I ran around in panic, trying to write down the addresses and telephone numbers of our parents. Jon promised to contact them, by telephone or postcard, to inform them of our situation and let them know that we were alive, safe, and as well as could be expected.

President Saddam Hussein had given permission for elderly Frenchmen, and those in ill health, to go home to France. Poor Marc was too young to join his countryman. We all felt so sorry for him, but maybe this was a step in the right direction.

Jon shook my hand one more time and kissed me on both cheeks: "You take care." Although he was happy to be going home, he was very sad for those left behind.

Jon was escorted outside into the darkness, to an awaiting Land Rover. He would be flying home on Monday. We all waved good-bye, fending off the mosquitoes, as the tears rolled down my cheeks. We watched the Land Rover as it disappeared into the distance.

Whenever anyone left, we all felt a great sense of loss, even Jay, who had constantly bickered with the French about the Second World War, causing lots of animosity. We sat in the main room, found some tea we had hidden, and brewed up. We sat listening to the two am broadcast on the BBC. It confirmed that Saddam Hussein was allowing the release of some French nationals, men over sixty and the sick. President Mitterrand declared that France would send more troops to the Gulf and Prime Minister Margaret Thatcher stated that although she had sympathy for the hostages and their families, they would not tolerate terrorists or aggressors. In South Africa, Nelson Mandela made a speech with regards to the massacre in the black townships.

We sat up talking, drinking tea and smoking until half past four. Rob appeared with a half bottle of Scotch that he generously shared around. I declined, as I'm not a Scotch drinker.

Sunday 16th September 1990.

We didn't manage to get up for the *Gulf Link* broadcast, but it was just as well as apparently it is not broadcast on Sundays. Chris and I surfaced to the aroma of food and were not surprised to discover it was chicken again, probably the same as that we'd been served the night before. Someone had kindly placed our chicken in the fridge for us to eat later. The guards also arrived with pears, cucumbers and tomatoes that had all seen better days, but it was good to have some fresh food. Hot food always seemed to cause the diarrhoea.

I was impossibly tired and disorientated. Whenever I laid my head on the pillow, my thoughts reviewed the past forty six days, and worries about Sarah, Aisha and Noura. Were they safe? And what about the cats, Mush and Flash? Hopefully they had been released from the room at the Messilah Beach Hotel. I had visions of them trying to claw their way out, starving, with no food or water.

With the passing days, I had become ever more lethargic. My brain didn't function as it did when I was active and working. At the same time, it was awful to observe the men's strained faces slowly deteriorating, becoming thinner, paler and more subdued. They were all very worried about their futures, if and when they return home, and about what they would do. Would they be able to find work in the UK? Some of the middle aged men would probably be considered too old to hold similar positions to those they had had in Kuwait. All their plans and dreams had been destroyed.

Supper arrived. It was not chicken, but how we wished it was when we saw the alternative! We were given separate brown paper bags, each with a plastic white dish containing a cold hamburger, another piece of meat covered in some butter, a slice of dried cucumber and a sprig of parsley. It was totally inedible. I retrieved some cheese from the fridge and some bread and Chris and I made cheese on toast for everyone. There was enough for one piece of toast per person, and it went down extremely well, but some of the men were still hungry and even tried to eat the hamburgers, adding lots of soy sauce for flavour. After the meal, the table was scattered with white plastic dishes, most of which were still full.

*

We all sat in the main room. I read, while the men played cards. The men were becoming agitated with one another and looking for any excuse to have a go at someone. It became almost impossible to concentrate, so I escaped to our room to read in peace. At around one in the morning there was lots of shouting in Arabic outside in the corridor. I opened the door to see Mr Ahmed, the big boss, walking around with one of the armed guards. It was quite amusing, as the guards had been caught unawares. He had caught them sleeping in the security area, which was in darkness apart from the light of a TV. Cassim came from his room rubbing his eyes, looking sleepy and disorientated. Mr Ahmed pointed to the main room. There were still plastic dishes and dirty cups all over the table. He shouted at the soldiers to clean up, and then went to inspect the kitchen. Within minutes, the rubbish had been removed and the toilets were cleaned.

"I would like to ask how things are," Mr Ahmed told me. "What is the food like?" As he waited for an answer, he went to check the fridge and shouted at the guards to remove some old perishable food. I took the opportunity to say what I thought. Mr Ahmed seemed a reasonable sort of man and, through the translator, he tried to explain about the reduction in our food quantities and that we had to suffer as their people were suffering. I asked why food should be wasted when all we needed was bread and cheese.

"I wouldn't give our food to a dog!" Chris butted in.

Although it was quarter to two, Chris knocked on the doors of those sleeping to say that Mr Ahmed would like to discuss our situation and we all assembled in the main room.

"Can we communicate with our families?" we begged. After all, we had not asked to come to Iraq. As usual, the answer was the same; we were there to keep peace and to prevent any intervention from the West. Chris pointed out that our governments would not change their views about using military force simply because we were there as hostages. Mr Ahmed appeared totally confused about some of our questions. Mr Sezuki asked for a bottle of whiskey via the Japanese Embassy, but we would have to wait and see.

After Mr Ahmed's departure, we sat up talking well into the morning. Mr Ahmed had said we would not be moved; this would be our guest-house until we returned home.

Earlier in the evening, Mr Bush's speech to the Iraqi people was shown on Iraqi TV and followed by a prearranged demonstration of the Iraqi people denouncing Bush's lies, burning the American flag and shouting, "death to Bush!" with vivid hatred. The message was shown in Arabic, and one of the guards walked over to the television set and spat on the TV once Bush had finished his speech.

Monday 17th September 1990.

We surfaced mid afternoon; lunch had been chicken once again.

It was interesting to see how many of the men found it calming to talk to a woman rather than the men. Quite often, the men would come and chat with me, discussing their worries and talking lovingly about their families. Today, we waited to see if our food situation would change. The night before, we had discussed the distribution of food and drinks with Mr Ahmed, and how receiving Pepsi was a real treat. Apparently, food and drinks should have been distributed to us. As we suspected, the guards had been helping themselves. They had been taking food and drinks outside, probably to their families. We would probably have done the same in such dreadful circumstances. We had all had our suspicions about the guards supplying us crap to eat while they kept the best. We knew that they bitterly hated the West, and as we were Western, we were, in their eyes, responsible for all their pain and suffering, so far as they could understand from what they were told under the Baghdad censorship. We harboured our thoughts on President Saddam Hussein, as the guards would not accept any derogatory or slandering remarks about him.

Cassim told me he had been working as a teacher in the university at the time of the invasion. A few days later, he was ordered to go to various installations as a translator. He was not allowed to contact his family, so in many ways he was in a similar situation to us.

Not a lot happened in Iraq. By now, I had lost faith in the news, especially the British broadcasts, as normally the only message from Margaret Thatcher was aggressive. Baghdad television informed us that she was inhumane and selfish with no concern for the hostages; a crazy woman whose evil was "against mankind."

Supper was as appetising as usual; some type of pastry, filled with meat, served with cucumber and stale bread rolls. Chris and I avoided it and had cheese and ketchup rolls. There was a definite chill in the air. People were becoming obsessive over food, food quantities and drinks. This was causing an unpleasant atmosphere and I hoped it would not escalate. Even now, some people were self-centred and only concerned with their own well-being.

The guards prepared one of the rooms as a kitchen for us to cook our own food; hopefully they would provide the food to allow us to do so. They had left us cabbage and eggs. Anything was better than what we had received to date.

*

That evening, we managed to tune into *Gulf Link*. Chris and I received a message from his parents and sisters wishing us well and informing us that the beers were lined up on the bar for our return. We felt lucky to get a message, as we had no idea if our families had received the letters we sent from Baghdad. But we were sure that the lucky ones who had been sent home had relayed messages to them. At least they did not have to rely on the foreign office. By now, Jay should have sent current, reassuring news about us.

It was another beautiful sunny day, so I decided to sit outside. Lunch was a waste of time; the kitchen was still in progress, and would possibly be finished tomorrow. Later that afternoon, I viewed a mouse bypassing the rat poison as I played Scrabble!

Before turning in for the night, the BBC told us that Iraqi diplomats had been expelled from Europe.

I should think so, too.

Tuesday 18th September 1990.

A knock on our door at eight in the morning summoned us to listen to the *Gulf Link* broadcast once again. Interference the night before had made it impossible to hear all the messages. I was still a little groggy from just three hours sleep. Although I had taken half a sleeping tablet kindly left by Jay, it had obviously not been effective. I just wanted *one* night of undisturbed sleep!

With a nice cup of hot tea, Chris and I sat listening once again to his parents' message, hoping it would come through loud and clear. It was a pleasant change to sit at the table for breakfast with BJ and Marc; we even had a boiled egg. Marc had heard Jon talking on the French radio station while in Amman in Jordan on his way home to France, saying that he had been well treated by his Iraqi "hosts". For obvious reasons, he would not discuss his experience in detail. Marc had come rushing into our room all excited to say Jon had arrived in France and to tell us about Jon's special message on the French radio station to his friends in Iraq. It cheered us up to know that Jon was safe at home with his family, probably having a nice drink and toasting us. It was also reassuring to know he would contact our families and tell them we were safe and well.

After the broadcast, I sat outside with Cassim, BJ, and Mr Sezuki, discussing the situation. I asked Cassim for some letter-headed note paper, showing Iraq. Chris and I had decided to write to Neil Kinnock at the Houses of Parliament, in the hope that he could arrange some sort of kind gesture in our favour. He appeared to be a compassionate man.

Carefully, I wrote:

To:

Mr Neil Kinnock - Member of Parliament.

As a British guest in Iraq, taken from Kuwait following the invasion on 2nd August 1990, I am writing to you in the hope that you personally, with your political influence and compassion, can help us in our plight by compromising with other European Countries to aim for a solution to the Gulf crisis. Although we are being extremely well looked after by the Iraqi government, we would desperately like to return home. Obviously I realise the task is great and will take time. Perhaps you could strive for negotiations with regard to releasing men in ill health, with on-going medical problems and also men over the age of fifty-five. Possibly you may consider a visit, acting as an envoy on behalf of the guests, to discuss with President Saddam Hussein releases on humanitarian grounds. As you are aware, some women have stayed behind with their loved ones, as I did. Perhaps you could talk on our behalf as well. I might add that it is very discouraging for all concerned to hear our own Prime Minister, with her blasphemous statements towards the Iraqi Government. As you are well aware, this does not help our situation; if anything it aggravates the issue.

We all want peace, not bloodshed and war. Please help.

In Anticipation.

Caroline Hughes.

On behalf of all men still in Iraq.

All letters were screened, so it was important to use diplomatic wording. We also thought of writing to newspapers; maybe in a day or two.

I decided to make some cheese and tomato on toast since we had processed cheese, fresh tomatoes and stale bread, which was ideal for toast. The men were more than enthusiastic about having something a little different to eat. I called it a "snack before supper". The major task was going into the revolting, filthy, smelly kitchen. As there was no grill, I used one of the two gas rings and a frying pan. I cut the tomatoes and cheese and placed them in the pan to heat a little, followed by the bread. It worked quite well considering, and once I had put it on a plate it looked quite appetising, with a garnish of cucumber and extra tomato.

<u>Wednesday 19th September 1990.</u>

Forty-nine days in captivity as "guests". How time flies when you're having fun! We were up bright and early to listen to the *Gulf Link*. I felt lucky to receive a message from a good friend, Robin, and from my family. It was a strange listening to my name on the radio and I felt a mix of emotions.

*

I sat with the men for breakfast and we spent two hours discussing various topics. The main topic on the agenda, of course, was Kuwait and Iraq. We discussed a British guest interviewed on TV, who had caused quite a stir. The man in question had been interviewed in a facility showing a swimming pool and tennis court. He was one of the fortunate oil workers in a compound not ruled by the Iraqis. He was basically under house arrest like the many others with him, and certainly not detained in any sort of installation.

The men were concerned that if this was shown on national television back home, the hostages would not be greeted with sympathy or approval from the British public. Unfortunately, we were not all receiving five star treatment. Sympathy would undoubtedly diminish if people thought we were in a holiday camp!

The BBC told us that the United Nations wanted an Air Embargo on Iraq. Baghdad TV showed coverage of a demonstration in London, outside the Houses of Parliament. It was held by students opposing the use of military force in the Gulf. Arab students from the UK and Ireland were also in the march. There was also news of the opposition party sending Members of Parliament to Baghdad to negotiate on our behalf, and to try and reach a peaceful solution to the current crisis.

Supper was actually quite edible and consisted of fresh fish, tomato, cucumber and "stone bread". Afterwards, the guards gave us permission to go outside the gate to jog around the perimeter of our abode. This decision was a bit of a shock, and of course we were chaperoned.

We found ourselves in a huge area, with lots of buildings resembling offices and laboratories surrounding us. We could see men and women wearing white coats walking between the buildings. Even though we were very discreet, the guards became very edgy whenever people came into view. The men also waved up in the air, hoping we would get picked up by satellite dishes trying to locate installations. Maybe someone would realise where we were. Needless to say, the guards were extremely nervous, and our trips outside the perimeter were very short lived. We managed to run a few laps. I was exhausted, but it was fun. Chris and the other men found it difficult to run in the extreme heat.

We could hear dogs howling in a building two or three hundred yards away, presumably from one of the chemical plants used for experiments. The howling was very disturbing, explaining the noises that we often heard in the early hours. I could only imagine the experiments.

Thursday 20th September 1990.

I tried to get up for the *Gulf Link*, but I just about managed to surface at midday after numerous cups of tea—to discover three mice running around the room! One was in the waste bin, one under the door and the third was coming out of the filing cabinet that we hid biscuits in. It was strange how I had become less frightened of them. I spent twenty minutes throwing anything within reach at them, including boxes of matches, but all to no avail. BJ and Marc suggested obstructing the two-inch gap under the door. They explained this to the guards, who finally blocked the gap with sponge.

Lunch was very impressive. The guards had cooked two boxes of rice and some type of soup stew. It was mainly lumps of fatty meat, but it tasted great compared to the recent culinary delights.

*

Chris was quiet and obviously fed up. I tried to keep him cheerful, but it was difficult. We all missed our families and wanted to go home. Sitting outside on the steps, I saw a Land Rover pull up at about four. In the back seat, sitting with three armed soldiers, there was a bearded man. He looked bewildered as he got out holding his plastic bag of goodies and a suitcase, but he was relieved to see other Europeans, and as he shook our hands he introduced himself as Diet, from Germany.

We now had one Frenchman, two Japanese, one American, five British and one German. I remembered the overwhelming relief in seeing other Europeans on being moved between installations.

The British men's nickname for Mr Sezuki was "Mr Toyota". Until now they had just used it discreetly, but it came out when Marc inadvertently asked "Mr Toyota" what he would like to eat. Mr Sezuki was red with embarrassment at first, but then he laughed. We all thought it was hilarious, and even Mr Sezuki saw the funny side of the joke, which helped to ease some tension. People still argued about silly things like other people's table manners and the Second World War, as Jay had done. We all tried to keep the peace by talking loudly about anything that came into our heads.

As I read, I took in the BBC news with half an ear. Iraq had been ousted from the Asian games, and South Africa had become everyone's priority. Apparently, the twenty seven countries involved in the Games had voted against Iraq joining in. The Kuwaiti team had arrived in Peking, and was displaying the Kuwaiti flag.

*

Supper was served in brown bags again. Inside each there was a white plastic dish containing six pieces of fatty meat, with "stone bread". BJ wanted to take a photograph as he said no one would believe what we were eating: "How they can expect men to survive on this is beyond me," he said, convinced that they were trying to starve us.

I went to see Cassim and asked for some tomatoes and cucumber. BJ and I followed him into the store room, where we saw that the fridge was stocked with Pepsi, milk, water, olives and melons. BJ made some soup from the fatty meat, adding tomato and cucumber. It was delicious along with a tomato and cucumber salad and the men were delighted.

The Iraqi news in English showed ten minutes of a demonstration of Iraqi children and mothers in London. The children were displaying Iraqi flags and some of the children held boards saying, "We love Daddy Hussein," as they chanted the same words. Although a democratic society offers freedom of speech, this was an absolute insult to all of us held in Iraq. Perhaps the British were trying to prove to Saddam Hussein that we allow freedom, regardless of the situation! The reaction from the men was heated, to say the least. They felt that we were being insulted, and that our government no longer felt that our situation was an issue. We were becoming an inconvenience. The media were not covering the hostage situation as before. Our fear was that if the British public was not frequently reminded of our situation we would be forgotten and eventually killed. Clearly, our government was trying to play down our plight.

Friday 21st September 1990.

We were up bright and early to listen to the *Gulf Link*. Chris received a message from his parents saying that they had received his letters. The thought that all our families might have received our letters cheered us up. Many people appeared relatively happy today as we had our usual cups of tea.

The *BBC World News,* on the other hand, told us that Iraq would not agree to withdraw from Kuwait. Saddam Hussein declared that he believed Iraq would win the struggle. Iraq expelled military attaches in Baghdad from France, Germany and Spain and Thatcher had said that this was unjustifiable. There was a ban on new Iraqi nationals going to the UK, including students, although students who were already there would not be affected.

One of the guards said that President Saddam had told his people to prepare for war. As we stewed over that, lunch was prepared by a lady whom we nicknamed "Madame Fiona"; stew with rice.

*

I was fed up. The news was ever more discouraging. I wasn't the only one. The men even asked the guards if they would shoot us if Iraq was attacked by the USA. The guards were surprised, and told us that they were here to serve us. But of course they would have to follow orders it they were told to shoot us. The guards were totally unaware of the European forces against them and had no idea about air force weapons. All they knew was that there was a huge army of men prepared to fight until the end. Unfortunately for them, their only exposure to global events came from the heavily censored television.

Chris had become very subdued. He was worried about my being there, and what would happen to me if Iraq was attacked by the USA. What if we were separated?

"You're to take the next available flight home!" he told me. I was confused and scared. What would happen to us if the shit hit the fan? So far, we had been lucky and, even in a bizarre situation like this, we had moments of passion. It was obvious to everyone that we were very much in love, but the strain was growing, especially now that war was inevitable. Through it all, Chris continued to be caring and protective.

*

Later that evening, Rob called us into his room to show us a large, plastic talcum powder bottle. He emptied the contents onto the bed. Sprays of white powder fell out, along with lots of small one gram bars of gold! We stared in amazement. Rob had worked in a dental laboratory, and when the Iraqis invaded he decided to take his salary, hiding the gold bars in his talcum powder. He had a few bottles, all containing the gold used for fillings. We all had a good laugh about Rob's clever thinking!

We left Rob's room to find a letter from the British Embassy:

Caroline Hughes Myers

British Embassy

BAGHDAD. September 1990.

Dear Fellow Countrymen,

I am sorry I am unable to make direct contact with you, but I should like to assure you by this letter that the British Government are doing everything they can to make it possible for you and other British citizens to leave Iraq.

I hope that you and fellow detainees are as well as the circumstances of your detention permit. The Iraqi authorities have constantly assured us that you would be safe and well treated. We have been doing what we can to press that indeed your living conditions should be good. One small advance has recently been registered in that the authorities have established a channel (by setting aside a Post Office Box NUMBERS 39090 50300 and 50285) through which letters can reach you. It seems clear from our experience that if you for your part write letters, the Iraqi authorities will pass them to us: we of course pass them as quickly as we can. (Which admittedly has not been fast in recent weeks)

I expect you know the BBC World Services are now broadcasting a program called   'Gulf Link' which is used to relay personal messages from the United Kingdom.

The program is broadcast twice a day- from 0445 to 0500 GMT on 111760, 15245 and 17815 kHz and from 1645 to 1700 GMT on 6040, 11720 and 15120 kHz.

I enclose a list of Current BBC World Service frequencies in the hope that you do in fact have access to a radio.

Yours sincerely

British Ambassador.

Saturday 22nd September 1990.

Unfortunately, we missed the *Gulf Link* broadcast, after getting to sleep around five thirty. One of the men had received a message from his wife; it was always so comforting to see the happiness on people's faces whenever a message got through.

The *BBC World Service* was as depressing as ever. The thought of war terrified me. Chris took me in his arms.

"You're going home on the next available flight that they arrange for women," he said firmly. I cried. Half of me wanted to go, but the other half was still undecided. I felt guilty at the thought of leaving Chris and the others behind. We sat huddled together for maybe an hour while I cried, terrified to go with the guards on my own.

Apparently, Chris spoke to the guards this morning, telling them that they may just as well shoot us as it would stop the uncertainty. The torment of pondering what may happen eventually was becoming unbearable. He had also decided that it would be safer for me to get out. Neither of us knew how things would work out.

Not one day had passed without Chris trying to be protective, reminding me to tie my hair up and cover myself in baggy shirts and tracksuit bottoms. Although some of the guards were pleasant enough, we couldn't trust them.

It was true that if I left, I could be of more benefit to the men in the UK. At least I would be able to relay messages to their families and make sure the British public did not forget about them. All the men were in agreement, as they were all concerned for my safety.

*

While we thought about all this, Chris cooked amazing fried rice to go with the bagged chicken for supper while I helped chop up tomatoes and cucumbers to add to it. It was a great improvement on the food we had been having. The guards arrived with Pepsi, oranges and chocolate bars and were impressed with our culinary efforts.

Later, Chris spoke to one of the guards regarding the possibility of my going home. The guard said that first he would have to inform the necessary officials. After some hours, he informed Chris that the officials had agreed, but that I would have to write a letter to the Iraqi authorities to confirm that I wanted to leave. The letter would then be passed on to the necessary authorities for the final decision. Apparently, a flight would be leaving in two to three days with the military attachés who had been expelled from Kuwait. Mr Seguchi gave me letters for his family, telephone numbers of work offices and family addresses in Japan. He also gave me $25, which I finally accepted at his insistence, along with $20 that Mr Sezuki gave me. They asked me to promise them that I would use the money to have a couple of beers for them. The other men took it in turn to give me addresses, telephone numbers and messages and letters to be passed on to their loved ones. We all became very emotional. Through our shared experiences, we had developed a bond that no one else could share or even understand.

"Shout from the rooftops," I was told, "and contact the newspapers to make sure that we are not yesterday's news!"

I hoped that my prayers would be answered and that I would be allowed to go home and fight for the men. Chris sat with me as I wrote the letter asking permission to leave:

Iraqi Authorities. 22nd   September 1990.

To whom it may concern,

I am writing this request to you in the hope that you will be able to arrange for my departure to England at your next opportunity.

This request is being made on the assumption that the gesture made by President Saddam Hussein, stating that women and children may return to their home countries, still stands. I have been assured by the officials looking after us that it does.

I have decided to make use of the gesture now, after discussions with my husband, only because I know my family will be extremely worried about me, and with the knowledge that my mother is unwell. I do not want to cause her unnecessary stress. Of course I would be extremely grateful if you were to allow my husband to depart with me, as I know life at home will be difficult without him. I do however realise this may not be possible, but if you could allow him to travel with me to the last stopover point before I depart, I would again be most grateful.

Finally, both my husband and I would like to take this opportunity to thank President Saddam Hussein and the people of Iraq for their hospitality in these difficult times, ever since we arrived from Kuwait to Baghdad at the beginning of August. I would also like to say that I will be writing to Prime Minister Margaret Thatcher on my return to the UK to express my extreme disapproval of her conduct and handling of Britain's intervention of the present situation in the Gulf.

Yours sincerely.

Caroline Hughes.

The guards took the letter away. It was over the top, but I knew that this was what the authorities wanted to read. If this was what it took to go home, so be it! Now it was time to wait for a reply. All I could do was hope that the answer would be what I wanted to hear.

While I waited, we all talked about having a big reunion on the men's return and agreed my approach. I would have to be diplomatic, so as not to antagonise the Iraqis. I didn't want to be responsible for any hostilities towards the men. After being here for so long, I understood our guards' mentality. It was almost like dealing with children, trying to be the diplomat without offending anyone. The guards firmly believed in what they were doing. They thought that they were helping to avert war and protect their country.

Sunday 23rd September 1990.

We received a message from Chris' family on *Gulf Link* telling us to keep our spirits up, but I was a little disappointed not to receive a message from my family. Later, however, I found out that the letter I presented to the guards was under discussion. In a day or two, I might be taken to the Melia Hotel for an exit visa, passport and whatever details had to be completed before I could leave Iraq. I kept asking if Chris could come with me just for the journey, as I was terrified at the thought of travelling in a Land Rover with the armed guards. I was desperately sad and confused; guilty about leaving without the men, perhaps never to see Chris or the rest of them again. Part of me wanted to stay, but they all insisted that I could help them much more at home. The translators were happy that I had decided to leave.

"It's the right decision," said one of them, Jaffa. "The uncertainly about war is making the situation very tense."

I just hoped I would be able to achieve some hope for the others by contacting their families. BJ came with another note for his family on a tiny piece of paper for me to put somewhere inconspicuous and Diet and Rob followed with more notes and telephone numbers.

"Send us a message on *Gulf Link* when you get back," they urged, "so that we know you have arrived home safely."

Before I left, Jaffa arrived with a bright blue tracksuit for my journey. It was a kind gesture. The men laughed as it was a shell suit, and they made me promise to wear it on arrival at Heathrow. We called it the "Hostage Suit". At least it added a few pounds to my now very thin frame. The constant diarrhoea had made the weight fall off me; another reason for Chris wanting me to leave. The Baghdad Diet had a lot to answer for!

All we could do now was wait for the final decision on my release. My heart was breaking and I was consumed by guilt.

<u>Sunday 30th September. 1990.</u>

The past few days had been like an eternity. Sometimes, I had even hoped that the Iraqis would refuse to let me go. Until now, it had seemed that that might be the case.

Chris and I were playing Scrabble in our room at around ten at night, when a guard came to the door, avoiding eye contact.

"She's been given permission by the Iraqi authorities to leave," he told Chris. "Tell her to get ready. She's to go immediately. The transport is waiting outside."

I blanched and started to shake and cry.

"Can't it wait until the morning?" Chris begged.

"No," the guard replied. "You have ten minutes."

Chris hugged me. He tried to hide his fear, but it was still evident. He unfastened the gold chain he was wearing and put it around my neck.

"Look after this for me, and give it to me when I get home." He also handed me a letter that he had written days before for me to open when safely on a flight home to the UK.

On hearing the commotion, the other men had come out of their rooms.

"You're doing the right thing, Caroline," they insisted. I was to go home and try to keep the hostage situation in the public eye. They also insisted that I wear my blue "Hostage Suit" as a memory of our times together! As I left, they were still handing me small bits of paper with names, addresses and telephone numbers. We all knew that most people trying to leave through Saddam International Airport had anything of value stolen by the Iraqi airport staff; small pieces of paper would be more likely to make it through. Ten minutes later, the guard arrived. All the men lined the corridor to give me a final hug with tears in their eyes. It was heartbreaking. They followed me out to the Jeep. Standing alongside it were four military men with their guns, in full green uniform. For a moment, I thought it was the end. They could take me anywhere and nobody would know. Chris had to stay on the steps with the others so I held back for a final hug. As we embraced, he told me through his tears that he loved me, and that I should contact him via the *Gulf Link* as soon as I arrived. He would have no other way of knowing that I was safe.

With tears streaming down my face, I followed the armed guards. I desperately tried not to show my fear, but my body trembled as I clutched onto my black bin liner containing the papers on which I had been writing my diary every day. I carried Chris' briefcase and wore his gold chain.

Just before I climbed into the Jeep, I looked around at the men standing at the main entrance, one final time.

"Get in the back," one military officer told me. One officer sat beside me, one sat in the driver's seat and the other in the passenger seat. As we started to move, I tried to turn around to see the men at the door, but the windows were covered. I sat sobbing while the officers talked and joked. We travelled over dirt tracks in darkness. I expected the worst. I had gone into shock and felt totally drained. I prayed that I would get to Baghdad safely, but that if I didn't that the end would be quick. How I wished I had stayed at the camp with the protection of the men! The Iraqi guards enjoyed my fear as they drove around narrow lanes. After about forty minutes, the roads displayed signs for Baghdad. Now I had hope; perhaps they *were* taking me to the Mansour Melia Hotel!

After over an hour, the Jeep stopped at the hotel. I was asked to get out and follow two of the guards through the back entrance. It was a very familiar sight, as it had been my first introduction to Baghdad many weeks before. Eventually, we were met by another guard in civilian clothes who told me that he was going to take me to a room. I followed him into the lift to the fifth floor and followed him along the corridor, arriving at a door that he unlocked with a key. He passed me the key and told me to go in and wait until someone contacted me.

Still scared, I walked into the room. It was a normal hotel bedroom, with twin beds and a telephone on the bedside table. I sat on the bed wearing my blue "Hostage Suit", totally drained. After thirty minutes or so the telephone rang, making me jump. At first I was reluctant to answer it, but after a few minutes I picked up the receiver.

"Hello?" I said, hesitantly.

I was relieved to hear a British accent on the other end. It was an official from the British Embassy in Iraq. He said that he was unable to access my room, but had been granted permission to meet me downstairs.

Shortly afterwards, a guard came to escort me downstairs. I followed him into the secured lobby area, well away from other visiting "guests" representing their various humanitarian causes. As I arrived, the man from the British Embassy stood up and shook my hand. The guard left us alone. The relief of finally meeting with someone in a position to get me home was overwhelming and I broke down in tears, eventually composing myself enough to sit and listen.

"Caroline, you are still not entirely safe," the man told me, "as the secret police are observing everyone and the telephone lines are tapped. You'll need to keep a low profile and avoid discussion of your treatment with anyone. If you must do it, to be very diplomatic and do not say anything derogatory about Iraqi hospitality. You will have to stay in Baghdad for a few days so that we can finalise exit permits and a passport, but we have obtained permission for you to be transferred to the Hotel Palestine, where all the foreign journalists are staying. I want you to come with me now, before they change their minds."

At that, I was escorted up to my room to collect my belongings. I quickly grabbed my black bin bag and Chris's briefcase, which I noticed had been moved. Clearly, the secret police had been checking it.

The Embassy official had arranged a car but he was unable to travel with me as we were still under Iraqi rule. Instead, we were to meet at the Hotel Palestine. I knew that I was still not out of harm's way, and was scared by how quickly everything was happening.

The driver, an official Iraqi in civilian clothes, drove around Baghdad. In about fifteen to twenty minutes I arrived at the Hotel Palestine. By now, I was paranoid and too scared to make eye contact with anyone. The Embassy official was waiting.

"I've organised a room for you," he told me efficiently, "and will telephone later and arrange for a diplomatic car to collect you so that you can meet with some people from the British Embassy." Once again, I was escorted upstairs, where I was handed the key to a room. I closed the door, locked it and put on the safety chain.

Then I noticed that, above my head, the ceiling had white partitions with gaps in between them. I became convinced that these gaps contained hidden cameras from the secret police, and grew even more paranoid and scared.

Would I ever leave Iraq?

I sat on the bed for a moment and then moved to the balcony because I felt that someone was watching me. It was probably just paranoia, but I found some relief in sitting cross-legged on the balcony floor, overlooking normal night time activity in Baghdad. I could see the bright lights of cars driving and hear their horns. I was lonely, frightened and exhausted. I knew that I looked an absolute sight and hardly recognised my thin body. My eyes were swollen from the continual crying and fear was written all over my face. The diarrhoea had started once again, along with my period, and once again I was in desperate need of some provisions. I showered quickly, convinced the cameras were observing my every move, and made do with tissues. There were other British "guests" staying in the Hotel Palestine, also waiting to go home on humanitarian grounds because of ill health. The former British Prime Minister, Edward Heath, had been negotiating on their behalf.

It was close to midnight when the telephone rang so loudly that I jumped.

"Come downstairs," I was instructed. "A car is waiting for you."

I reluctantly removed the chain from the door, unlocked it and went towards the lift. When I arrived at the ground floor, the Embassy official shook my hand and escorted me to the diplomatic car. It was still safe to travel in a diplomatic car, but that might not be the case for much longer. I was driven to a private residence to meet with various officials who wanted to discuss what had happened to me. When we arrived, I met with a group of very pleasant British men who reassured me that, as soon as the paperwork for my passport and visa was ready, I would be free to go home. It would take perhaps three or four days.

My heart sank; anything could happen. What if the Iraqis changed their minds, as they did so often? But there was nothing I could do. Of course, the British were still playing the diplomat and did not want to jeopardise the release of the ill and frail, while negotiations were still taking place.

I was asked a lot of questions: Did I know about the various chemical installations I had been imprisoned in? Did I know where they were? They also wanted information on all the Iraqi military we had met over the last sixty days or so, going into the details of their uniforms and individual names. I was asked what activity I had observed, and what was used, such as military weapons and tanks. Finally, I was asked for the names and nationalities of the men held with me.

As I answered their questions, we sat in a beautiful garden surrounded by trees at a table laid with a fantastic selection of food. I could only manage some chicken and bread, as my stomach was not ready for such abundance. Still, it was nice to look at it and I did accept a cool, crisp glass of dry white wine. I raised my glass for Chris and the guys; that one was for them. The wine went straight to my head and produced a welcome sensation of numbness.

Before I left, one of the officials gave me some serious advice: "Keep a low profile in the Hotel Palestine; the secret police are active and observing all activity at the hotel and even the phone lines are tapped. Expect them to enter your room and look around when you are not there. We suggest you stay in your room with the door locked and wait for a call from an Embassy official. Only leave the room to go to breakfast in the morning."

Before I left, I had an important request: "Can I contact my parents?"

The Embassy official said he would be able to arrange a call for the following day.

By now, morning had come and I was exhausted. The diplomatic car arrived with the chauffeur to drive me through Baghdad back to the hotel. I felt as though I was in a James Bond film, and wished that it was all just a bad dream.

Back at the hotel, I kept my head down, finally getting into my room, locking the door and putting on the safety chain. It was almost two in the morning. I lay on the bed with my head spinning from a mixture of the events and the wine, finally falling asleep fully clothed. I woke at about seven to noise coming from everyday activity outside.

Thank God I had survived another day! The telephone rang and I was informed that breakfast was being served. After a shower, I selected a change of clothes from my black bin liner. I pulled out a blue shirt that belonged to Chris and black tracksuit bottoms and tied my hair back in a pony tail. I unlocked the door and made my way via the lift to the breakfast room where I found Europeans from various different places. Everyone seemed to be staring intently at me, and I felt uncomfortable. I made my way towards a table in the corner and a kind, jovial woman came over and introduced herself. I discovered that her husband was going to be one of the fortunate men to be released on health grounds through the help of Edward Heath. He was very ill with a brain tumour.

I had been advised by the Embassy officials to be diplomatic and discreet if the media started asking questions. Obviously, I should take care not to tell the whole truth about the camps as it was still a delicate issue, and the Iraqi regime did not accept any derogatory statements.

Eventually the whispering began. All the other "guests" wanted to know where I had appeared from and what my story was. I supposed it was natural for them to be curious. A TV journalist asked me if I was okay and whether I needed anything. I just burst into tears, much to my disgust. I seemed to be out of control; I felt vulnerable, and so frightened of saying the wrong thing.

"Do you think you could get me some tampons?" I asked, composing myself, and avoiding going into detail about where I had appeared from. She said that she could and I retreated nervously to my room.

Shortly thereafter, the journalist arrived with the tampons. What a great relief! I asked her to check the partitions above her head to see if she could see any hidden cameras. She couldn't and tried to reassure me it was fine. Realising I was a little delicate, she came into the room and told me not to worry.

"You are perfectly safe here," she said. But I was growing ever more paranoid. It was a bit like being a caged animal, always being observed and followed everywhere. And now, suddenly, I was free. Naturally, the journalist was curious about what had happened to me. I thought about the men in the camps and how they had asked me not to let the British public forget about them. I decided that I could use the situation to my advantage, without disclosing too many details; just enough to get the attention of the media.

The journalist was happy to get some sort of story and went to work. I had absolutely no idea of what the media had covered about human shields in the past months. Apparently it was becoming old news, but here I was and they were ready to cover the topic again from a new angle. I was someone new and fresh from the installation, and a female. They asked me to visit an oil compound in Baghdad with them, where men were virtually under house arrest, scared to venture out in case they were taken hostage.

The men were basically free, with all facilities. They had a swimming pool, tennis courts and a bar fully stocked with alcohol. At first I couldn't believe it; it looked like a holiday camp! Of course the people back home were not going to be sympathetic! I was angry, as it was so different from the reality many were experiencing. I would have to portray a different image, in a very diplomatic way, but with enough detail to get media attention.

Back in the room, I received a call to say the international line was free. As I dialled my parents' telephone number, my hands shook. I tried to control my emotions, telling myself not to cry. I had not seen my family for over a year, and hadn't spoken to them since the invasion, so they had no idea if I was alive or dead.

My sister-in-law, whom I knew to be heavily pregnant by now, answered the phone.

"Hi Jet," I said, "it's Caroline. Can I speak to Mum?" I could hear the shock in Jet's voice as she asked where I was and if I was alright. I just burst into tears, and Jet started screaming for my mum to answer the phone.

For what seemed like an eternity, Mum and I both cried, unable to speak. Eventually, I composed myself and said that I was fine, awaiting a visa and passport in Iraq and that I would be allowed to leave in a few days. It was such a nice warm feeling to hear my mother's voice and I just wanted her to put her arms around me and tell me that everything was going to be alright.

Then the line went dead.

*

The Embassy had arranged for me to visit a residence later that evening, to meet with more officials. Again, I was taken in a diplomatic car. I arrived at what appeared to be a cocktail reception. Most of the people there were men in dinner suits, as most women and children had left Iraq at the start of the conflict. Initially, I was angry. How could they entertain with such little consideration for the men in the camps who had little food and were living in appalling conditions? There were waiters walking around with trays of wine, for God's sake! Chris and the other men would have been horrified if they could have seen it.

The officials promised to try and send certain provisions through the Iraqi government to the men. I suggested that a few beers would be very welcome. After a long and tedious evening answering questions and feeling a little worse for wear as the wine took effect, I was driven back to the Hotel Palestine. Sitting in the lobby, there was a journalist from a well known London newspaper, waiting to pounce. It was now well after midnight and he asked me to join him for a drink, wanting a story. We agreed that he would print the story on the day I left for Iraq. For now, I was reluctant to talk. I had to protect the men and would have to continue with the line that Chris and I were married, for fear of any reprisals. I later discovered that journalists often make things up.

Media from all over the world, including the BBC, were at the hotel. TV AM had asked me to allow them to film me once I received my passport and ticket and to follow the story back home on my arrival. I agreed; this would be my way of speaking on behalf of Chris and the others. Being in the limelight was a totally unreal experience and very out of character for me, but I was still horrendously guilty about having left the men. We had a bond and understanding that no one else could have understood.

Meanwhile, the Embassy asked if I would be willing to take a diplomatic bag with me to hand over to an Embassy official in Amman, Jordan on my journey home.

*

Finally, my papers and documentation had been approved. I was taken to Saddam International Airport with a driver and translator. The airport was in chaos; people were desperate to leave Iraq, as war was imminent. Everyone knew that belongings were often stolen by the customs and police. The Indian people in particular were treated very badly. Suitcases were opened and belongings thrown on the ground for them to pick up. I commented on the translator's gold watch with a picture of Saddam Hussein on the face. He proudly said it was a gift from Saddam for his loyal service. I clutched the diplomatic bag tightly. I had put my handwritten notes into the bag; the notes I had started to write about my experience since the invasion. The translator pushed through the crowds of people showing my visa and passport and ticket for Amman, Jordan, and then to the UK.

The coast was still not clear. I had to go into a booth with some rather large Iraqi policewomen, who were free to search me and steal whatever took their fancy. They were unpleasant. One frisked me while another looked through my bin liner and the diplomatic bag. The one frisking me held onto the gold chain that Chris had asked me to keep safe. Thankfully, she had second thoughts about taking it, and let it go as they ushered me through. Fortunately, the diplomatic bag was of little interest to them.

Having gone through the barrier, I waved to the translator to thank him. As I entered the airport lounge, I saw people lying on the ground. There were bodies everywhere. I managed to find a corner to sit in. Tears streamed down my face as I pleaded with God to let me go.

After a couple of hours, I finally boarded a flight to Jordan, but I didn't feel safe until that plane left the runway!

*

In Jordan, I was met by another Embassy official who thanked me for the diplomatic bag and passed me on to another official. We had to walk quickly to get the UK flight as it was due to leave immediately. I was escorted onto the flight with the Embassy official in tow and shown to a seat at the back. As I listened to the noise of the engine preparing to take off, I finally realised that I really was going home. For most of the five or six hour flight, I sat at the back with cathartic tears streaming down my face.

I opened the letter Chris had given me and read it:

3 pm Sunday September 1990.

Darling Caroline,

I hope you saved this letter and are now en route to England. You don't know what it has meant to me, the fact that you have stayed with me since the first women and children left. I guess it was confirmation that you love me. I hope so because I know you mean everything in the world to me. I'm sorry I can't come with you, but as we discussed you have got plenty to do when you get home. As you know I'm still very confident of all of us getting out of here safely and the fact that you will be waiting for me will keep me going.

I'm looking at your photograph now and will be doing so every day until I see you back home.

Remember, don't read too much into the rubbish printed in the papers at home and promise me you will go and see my family. I know they would love to see you.

As I said, please contact me through the Gulf Link as soon as you arrive because I will not sleep until I know you're home safely.

I know it's the right thing to do and I promise I will buy you an engagement diamond ring when I get home.

Finally, don't worry about me, I can look after myself. Anyway gorgeous I'll sign off now and let you have another beer or whatever you're drinking now.

I already miss you, keep your chin up.

I love you darling.

Chris. x

October 4th 1991.

I arrived at Heathrow, wearing my "Hostage Suit". I had been told that the Ministry of Defence would be contacting me to discuss the last couple of months in Iraq. On arrival, I was escorted through the airport to the blinding lights of television cameras. Standing in the corner, holding flowers, was my family. They all came running towards me and hugged me as they cried. It was overwhelming. My three sisters hugged me to death and my Mum and Dad were so relieved to have me back! One of my sisters was holding a copy of the *Evening Standard* with my face and story on the front page. The journalist in Baghdad had kept his promise not to print it until I was on the way home.

The house was filled with balloons to welcome me home, but I was still thinking about all the men and how to ensure that they wouldn't be forgotten. I had arranged to go on TV AM the following morning. It was hard for me to concentrate because I felt so very guilty about having abandoned Chris and the others. I had to help them however I could, and if that meant involving the media, so be it.

Desperate to explain to my family all about the past days in Iraq, I couldn't stop talking. I was totally exhausted, but I had to contact all the men's families to give them a glimmer of hope and send the letters. As you can imagine, their relief was immense. I also had to contact Chris' parents, who had never met or spoken to me. We had planned to meet the families that summer, before the events in Kuwait. Needless to say, his family was desperate to meet me, and to get any information they could about Chris. I discovered that my family had received very little information about where I was. The Foreign Office had told them that I had remained in Kuwait. On the August Bank Holiday Monday, they learned that I was actually in Iraq as we had been shown on television. They had been relieved that I was alive and not in Kuwait as they had been led to believe. The news had been shown all over the international circuit and most of the newspapers had followed the story. In fact, Chris and I had been plastered all over the newspapers, because I had been unable to speak and had burst into tears. Although it had been very difficult for my family to see this, they had been grateful I was alive.

October 5th 1991.

I was still frightened. The night before, I slept in my parents' bedroom on a camp bed, too scared to sleep alone. I had started to suffer from nightmares, waking up in a panic, convinced the guards were still following me, trying to take me back to the camps. After a few hours, it was actually a relief to get up. I still felt dazed, almost as if I'd been drugged.

TV AM had arranged for a driver to pick me up from my parents' house at five in the morning, to appear on breakfast TV. This was a continuation of the initial interview in Baghdad, using the angle of a woman separated from her man. I had to borrow clothes from my mother and sisters because I had dropped from ten to six and a half stone. I decided on a shirt which had to be pinned at the back as it was falling off me, and a shirt and jacket. I was driven to the TV AM studio in London. It was a totally bizarre situation. I didn't feel nervous, just numb, and felt that the interview was a duty I owed the men still in Iraq. Under normal circumstances, it would have been very exciting to appear on television.

I knew that I was fortunate to have the opportunity to try to make a difference, and was totally convinced that I had been given a second chance at life. My parents respected my decision to go on television, although my mother found it difficult. The interview was nothing special, although I did have the opportunity to speak on behalf of the men, and ensure they were not put to the bottom of the pile. Without insulting the Iraqi government, people had to know that they were not in holiday camps! It was amazing to meet and see all the famous TV presenters, who were all so kind.

Later, officials from the Ministry of Defence visited me at my parents' house, showing me photographs and books of weapons and tanks, asking me if I could identify any of them and whether I had seen them in Kuwait or Iraq. They also showed me aerial views of some of the installations that we had been kept in. Any information I could provide was helpful, but most of the time the view had been obliterated by screens and sheets. I gave the names of the Iraqi officials and described their uniforms, giving details of any decoration on their uniforms to indicate rank. Before they left, the officials advised me to go for a medical check up.

October 7th 1990.

I would need to have a medical report so that, at a later date, I could confirm the mental pain and anguish I had suffered, and I had been advised to see a counsellor or psychiatrist.

During the medical examination, I had to strip down to my underclothes.

"You poor girl, what did they do to you?" the doctor said when I undressed. He was looking at the dreadful bruises and the marks that the infected wounds from the sand flies and mosquito bites had left on my legs. Apart from these, and the weight loss, I was perfectly healthy. I refused to see a counsellor or psychiatrist. I was young enough to deal with the post-traumatic stress, with love and support from my family. I still had bouts of crying and was unable to sleep without the light on. I had recurring nightmares of the Iraqi soldiers taking me.

Maybe it was ridiculous to think that I could really change events and make a difference, but I was uncontrollably driven to do *something*. I had to follow my instincts, whatever the consequences. My main aim was to help the men. I still felt guilty, especially as I could understand how difficult the conditions in Iraq must be. I had been spending my days writing letters and telephoning government officials and had determined to march through London, in opposition to the war. My family had helped me put banners together and Chris' parents were going to join me. I had been asked to appear on CNN, BBC and Sky TV and would talk to anyone willing to listen. Together with my family, I had even stood outside the Iraqi Embassy in London, voicing my opinion.

October 25th 1990.

The news reported that Iraq had mined nearly half of Kuwait's 1,000 oil wells on the day that I received an unexpected telephone call from Sarah in Cairo. I had been trying to find out what had happened to her and the children. Fortunately, someone had read my story in a local newspaper, near John's home, and eventually John's mother contacted me to say that Sarah had finally managed to get to Egypt. We both cried as we talked, and Sarah was desperate for news about John. She wanted to come to England and leave the children with her family in Cairo. Within a few days she was on her way.

*

As my father and I drove to Heathrow to wait for Sarah's flight from Egypt, I was very excited at the prospect of seeing her after our parting in Kuwait.

Sarah walked through the arrivals lounge, looking as gorgeous as ever in her brown leather trouser suit, with enough luggage for a couple of months. We hugged and cried, talking incessantly.

"What on earth did they do to you?" she cried. "You look awful!" I was not quite a picture of my former self and she was surprised by how thin I had become.

As we drove back to my parents', I told Sarah that I had written to Edward Heath, Mr Neil Kinnock, Margaret Thatcher, Cardinal Basil Hume and the Archbishop of Westminster, asking the latter to join us on a visit to Iraq on humanitarian grounds to represent peace. I received very politically correct replies. The Cardinal felt that, as a Roman Catholic, he might not be accepted, although he had given the matter a lot of thought and prayer.

At the house, I showed Sarah the letter:

I am writing having just returned from Iraq, after being held as a British 'guest' since the invasion of Kuwait on August 2, 1990. I spent 64 days being transferred to various installation points. During this time our only source of information on the political situation in the Gulf was the BBC World Service News.

Fortunately, most people will never have to contemplate the anguish of myself, my husband and the other fellow "guests" whom I left behind. The Iraqi authorities granted me permission, eight days after my original request, to go home. The men and women remaining are hoping and praying that with public support the Gulf crisis shall conclude peacefully.

It is easy for the Government to state that it will not tolerate terrorist aggression. Would Mrs Thatcher and her colleagues encourage the same tactics if their families were held in an Iraqi installation?

We all realise this is an international situation, but we must ask ourselves:

Will sanctions be effective?

Who will they deprive?

The answer is, not only Iraqi women and children, but also our own country folk.

It may take years before any drastic effect descends on Iraq. I plead with the people of the UK not to forget our men in Kuwait and Iraq. Thanks to the visit of Edward Heath, many of the sick hostages have been released. What he has achieved is admirable on humanitarian grounds, not political. Edward Heath deserves respect and the support of the Government, regardless of their political grievances.

It may take months, possibly longer, for the hostages to return home. All the people who remain in Iraq have put their faith in those fortunate to have returned to the UK to make everyone aware of their plight, and not to become complacent with the issue.

Innocent people do not deserve to suffer for the financial gains of other nations.

Caroline Hughes Myers.

Sarah and I were both frustrated by the lack of support from the government.

Saddam Hussein had issued a public invitation for women to visit their husbands in Iraq for Christmas, and we had convinced ourselves that war would be avoided if women accepted this invitation; how could the British Government justify war, with innocent women travelling back to Iraq on humanitarian grounds? Sarah and I had both discussed this at length with our families, who thought that we must be suffering from Post Traumatic Stress Syndrome, and not be fully aware of our actions. As my family had never even met Chris, they thought that I had totally lost the plot. It took a while for them to understand just how strongly we felt about what we were about to do. We sat for hours around the kitchen table, trying to convince my parents.

Sarah and I travelled to London to the Iraqi Embassy where we met with a Mr Ibrahim, an Iraqi diplomat responsible for granting entry visas for Baghdad. Sarah and I discussed the situation with him and explained that we would enter Iraq as women delivering a message of peace.

"If you write a letter to President Saddam Hussein," Mr Ibrahim told us, "accepting his kind invitation to return to Iraq and give the letter to me, I will liaise with Iraq on your behalf."

3rd November 1990.

I penned the following letter for delivery to Mr Ibrahim:

To President Saddam Hussein.

I am writing to you in response to your invitation to visit our husbands in Baghdad for Christmas.

As I'm sure you are well aware, there is great controversy over this issue.

The British Government, Prime Minister Margaret Thatcher and the foreign office totally oppose the suggestion as propaganda tactics and are advising families not to accept this offer.

Regardless of their views and controversial policies, I and two other women would like to accept your offer to travel to Baghdad in the hope that you will consider meeting with us to discuss the release of our husbands. I am British, one woman is American, and the other is Egyptian, whose husband is a British Muslim.

We are not politicians and would be doing this on humanitarian grounds. I was one of your early guests, and stayed in various strategic sites before returning to the United Kingdom.

Since arriving back on 4th October 1990, I have publicly stated that, during my stay in Iraq, we were all very well treated by the Iraqi authorities and could not criticise the treatment. The three men in question were some of the early guests, taken two days after the invasion. Would you please consider releasing them?

The governments will be angry, and although we are not politically involved, we feel that as the governments are doing so little, it is up to us as women to voice our opinions.

This will embarrass our governments, especially if the visit proves successful. I was one of the fortunate ladies who received a telephone call from my husband, from one of the installations.

We will have television and national newspaper coverage to aggravate the government more.

Mr Edward Heath has written to me personally. He still maintains that a diplomatic solution, through negotiations, must be discussed. Mr Heath is against the government opposing our visit. He believes that we live in a free country, where no one has the authority to dissuade any of the families from going to Baghdad.

Please find enclosed letters that I have sent to:

Prime Minister Margaret Thatcher.

Mr Douglas Hurd.

Mr Neil Kinnock.

Mr William Walgrave.

Cardinal Basil Hume.

Local Members of Parliament.

National Newspapers.

Also enclosed is a photograph of my husband Chris, and myself, which was taken by the Iraqi authorities before we appeared on guest news on August 26th 1990. This was shown on national television. In the name of God and Peace, please consider our request.

The men in question are.

Mr Christian Mark Myers. British.

Mr John. British.

Mr BJ. American.

If we do visit, can you please guarantee our safe return home?

In anticipation,

Mrs Caroline Hughes Myers.

November 9th 1990.

In the morning, the news reported that the US would be sending another hundred and fifty thousand troops to Saudi Arabia, and that between four hundred and fifty and five hundred thousand American soldiers would be in place by mid January. This news made Sarah and I more determined than ever to visit our men in Iraq. We met once again with Mr Ibraham, who confirmed that the visas would be arranged. As we were going on humanitarian grounds, they were to arrange a meeting with the Iraqi Women's Federation once we arrived in Baghdad.

The television was to follow our journey in the UK prior to our visit; the more coverage we received the better for the men still in Iraq. Sarah and I prepared all the letters and names of organisations to contact through a Dr Farouk. We would be staying at the Mansour Melia Hotel, but this time I would be free, and Sarah's ability to speak Arabic would be a great advantage. Of course, we were frightened, because we did not really know what would happen. Sarah gave me encouragement and determination. We received news informing us that we would fly to Baghdad on the twenty-eighth of November. We would stop in Amman, Jordan overnight and fly to Iraq the following morning.

Wednesday November 28th 1990.

After a tearful farewell to my family at Heathrow, Sarah and I turned to wave as we walked through the departure gate. Our American companion had decided against going to Iraq, so there were just the two of us. We were treated with suspicion by the airport security and customs men; they must have been wondering why on earth we were going to Iraq, with war imminent. They checked our papers and passports numerous times and asked about our reasons for going. They were not very sympathetic to the cause. We arrived in Amman at night and were transferred to a hotel. Thank God Sarah spoke Arabic! The hotel was virtually dark, apart from low lighting in the corridors. Apparently this was normal in the current situation, to avoid being a target for missiles from Iraq.

Thursday November 29th 1990.

The news of the day informed us that the use of force to push Iraq out of Kuwait had been authorised. If Saddam didn't withdraw by the fifteenth of January, the Soviet Union would use force too, to protect its citizens in Kuwait.

Sarah and I had awoken to bright sunshine after a troubled night. We were both still a little apprehensive about our journey, but whenever we had doubts or were scared, we thought about the men who depended on us. We ate breakfast in the almost empty dining room, where only a few businessmen also dined.

Shortly afterwards, we were transferred to Amman Airport by the hotel transport. We were not in a position to see the wonders of Jordan! Soon, we boarded the flight for Iraq and Saddam International Airport. On the flight, we met some women who were travelling to Iraq for the same reasons. We all bonded immediately, and felt much safer in numbers.

On finally arriving in Iraq, we all felt very scared and vulnerable. We were met by officials, photographers and TV cameras. Once through the airport we were driven to our hotel, the infamous Mansour Melia. My heart sank. I had such vivid memories of the hotel, and they were not pleasant. Sarah held my hand and reminded me that we would be OK, because we were there under different circumstances. Sarah was right; we had letters to write and contacts to make. We had been given some information via the Iraqi Embassy in London about whom we should meet, and the name of a Dr Farouk who was contactable in the hotel.

In our room, we compiled a list of things we needed to achieve and get done:

1. Try to make contact with the Iraqi Women's Federation;

2. Portray the message of Peace with a letter stating our case;

3. Provide any letters and publicity pictures I had received at home (all details are important);

4. Meet with Dr Farouk;

5. Be willing to appear on Iraqi television and contact newspapers to organise going to the peace camp on Baghdad Island. Al Aras Island;

6. Meet with the Fellowship of Reconciliation (American).

After all that, we would need to collect all our details together. Then we would be in a position to ask Dr Farouk to arrange a meeting with the Iraqi Speaker of the National Assembly, Mr Sa'adi Mehdi Saleh. This was our main aim, as it was common knowledge that if you manage to meet with the speaker, the next meeting is likely to be with President Saddam Hussein.

"Maybe we'll get a gold watch with Saddam's portrait on the face!" we joked.

We arranged for one of the translators in the hotel to type a cover letter, briefly explaining our situation, plus a copy in Arabic. All the women asked me to be their spokesperson. They thought that I had a good understanding of the situation as I had been held with the men. The fact that I had returned to Iraq should also go in our favour. When the letter was completed, it read:

We are here in Iraq as a result of the generous invitation of President Saddam Hussein, in contrast to the wishes of our Governments who have totally opposed our actions. Regardless of their views and controversial policies, we have taken the initiative to return to Baghdad, having been here as guests. During that time, the treatment shown was of kindness and concern.

We have travelled from England as a group of five women to visit our husbands and to represent women in the same circumstances as ourselves.

We have come to show our endorsement of the peace initiatives of President Saddam Hussein. In addition to the personal reasons of our visit, we have come to portray the message of peace.

We are here on humanitarian grounds, not political. War is totally unacceptable as a means of settling differences between nations. The innocent people of Iraq do not deserve to suffer because of the political and financial aspirations of Western governments. We, as women, cannot rest when peaceful alternatives have not been fully explored. Collectively we have made strong impressions on our governments through our peace campaigns, via use of the media, national newspapers and radio. We have also attended marches in the name of peace.

We use our voices to declare the cause of true and ultimate peace. We are women with a common purpose, from different backgrounds and different circumstances. We all bring the same message of peace and wish for the release of our husbands.

Our campaign for peace will continue, through contacts at the Iraqi Embassy in London and with links from the Iraqi Women's Federation in Baghdad. Our men will also join us in this campaign.

Friday 30th November 1990.

On the news, it was reported that President Bush had invited Iraq's Foreign Minister, Tariq Aziz, to Washington and had offered to send the US Secretary of State, James Baker, to Baghdad. Meanwhile, many things had happened since our arrival in Baghdad. We met the ladies from Iraqi Women's Federation and presented them with donations of baby milk, which was being prevented from entering Iraq because of the sanctions being imposed. We sat with the Iraqi ladies, discussing our views on the situation, especially with respect to the children of Iraq. Everything was televised and many photographs were taken as we drank Arabic coffee and ate sweet dates with natural yoghurt. That evening, I received a call from the translator informing me that the men would be allowed to come and visit us in the hotel! They had watched us on Iraqi TV with the Iraqi Women's Federation. Chris later said that he had had no idea until that moment that I was back in Iraq. He thought we were crazy, but was also relieved.

As we got ready that evening, excited about seeing our men, Sarah and I decided to try out some face masks we bought in Amman made with black mud from the Dead Sea. We sat laughing at one another as the whites of our eyes peered through the black mud mask. It was hard to believe we were in such bizarre circumstances.

Finally the men arrived and we had a very tearful reception. I was not prepared for Chris' appearance; he had a beard and looked desperately thin and gaunt.

"After you left," he told me, "they sent me to another camp, where the conditions were horrendous." Chris had been staying in AL-Hadithah Air-Base, 200 kilometres north-west of Baghdad.

We all went into our separate rooms to have time alone. Chris and I sat hugging one another; he was still in shock about me arriving back after all we had been through.

"Well, you kept your word," he said with a smile, "you made sure we were not forgotten!" Then he looked at me and said, "What have you done to your hair? You've gone from brunette to a dreadful blonde colour!" When I had had my hair done, I had thought it was OK; the change had been part of my recovery.

We had our moment of passion and Chris told me how much he loved me. He told me that he knew when he first met me in Kuwait that I was different from the rest, but not as unconventional as this. We lay on the bed talking about our families and the political situation. The men had received little information about the current war situation. Chris thought we were crazy for coming back and worried that the Iraqis might change their minds at any time, as they had done before, and keep us against our will. After a couple of hours we all got together and ordered beers for the men; probably the best beer they had ever tasted! We sat up until the early hours and the men started to relax a little.

Afterwards, we met with the Iraqi organisation Peace and Coordination, and with the American Fellowship of Reconciliation-Peace campaigners. We were to be interviewed about our views. We also made televised peace messages for Iraqi television for Christmas and met with representatives from Iraqi newspapers and magazines.

Sunday 2nd December 1990.

All the women who had travelled to Iraq took part in a service for peace, which was televised for international TV. We showed our peace messages. The symbol of peace was a yellow rosette, worn worldwide. We managed to get yellow material from the souk and spent many hours trying to sew them together.

The service was very emotional, as the vicar representing the peace message was himself a hostage of Saddam. His daughter, one of our group, had travelled to Baghdad to see her father. Fortunately, the men had been allowed to remain with us in the hotel for a few days before being taken back to the camps. We sat in a makeshift church in a room in the hotel with chairs surrounding the altar. Tears streamed down our faces as we prayed for a peaceful conclusion to the crisis and displayed our yellow rosettes.

Monday 3rd December 1990.

In the *Baghdad Observer*, I read that the speaker of the National Assembly stressed Iraq's firm desire to bolster bilateral relations with all peoples of the world, especially with the French, to achieve peace and stability in the world away from the language of aggression and war. He was meeting with a French delegation of medical doctors visiting Iraq.

The men were told they would have to return to the camps to collect their belongings while we carried on with the peace group. We had another tearful goodbye, but felt confident we would all go home together. Collectively, we wrote to Saddam Hussein:

Dear President Saddam Hussein,

Following a meeting this morning with the President of the Iraqi Women's Federation, I am writing to you on behalf of the 10 ladies who attended. We are all from different backgrounds and have come from various situations.

As we explained to the Iraqi Women's Federation, most of us have husbands here who are official guests of Iraq. One lady's parents are here as guests. Our main aim is to request permission for them to travel with us back to our homes.

We have all travelled back to Iraq in defiance of our governments to try to prove that a peaceful settlement to the so-called 'Gulf Crisis' is possible through dialogue, and that peace is absolutely imperative.

Before returning to Baghdad last week, many of us have been heavily involved in Britain and other countries promoting the cause for peace because we truly believe that war would be a totally unacceptable means of settling these differences.

We also believe that depriving women and children of such vital commodities as food and milk is unacceptable. In response to this, we have asked the women's federation to accept a donation of baby milk on our behalf to promote our cause.

As you are aware, we are by no means diplomats and do not represent our governments. However, we hope that our token efforts to promote peace in the Middle East will help to convince the war-mongering governments of the West that war is not the way.

Yours sincerely,

Women's Peace Group

This letter was accompanied by a yellow rosette; the symbol of peace, and sent via Dr Farouk.

Following the letter, we received an invitation to meet with the Speaker of the Iraqi National Assembly, Mr Al Sa'di Mahdi Saleh. We were told to be prepared with our speech, and that transport would arrive to take us to meet with him.

*

We arrived at a very opulent government building, with Iraqi security everywhere. We were shown into a rather palatial building with typical ostentatious décor; lots of gold and marble and huge pictures of President Saddam Hussein throughout the corridors.

"Sit here," the official told us, and we took our place in a room alongside Russian business men, who were also waiting to see the speaker. We started to feel nervous when we saw all the men in uniform rushing around. I sat with Sarah, clutching the letters and papers we were to present in English and Arabic. I had asked Sarah, because of her Arabic background, but she insisted that the presentation should be from someone British, as we had travelled from England. The women had all voted for me to speak on everyone's behalf.

After lots of juices and Arabic coffee we were called into a huge room. There were chairs arranged in a semi circle around the main chair, and leads from cameras trailed on the floor. Cameras were set up throughout the room, and photographers were taking our photos. I sat on the left of the speaker's chair, only to be moved, as he liked the person to whom he spoke to sit on his right. Lost in thought, we awaited his arrival.

When the speaker finally came, he shook hands with everybody before he sat down. Bright, blinding lights from the cameras followed his every move. I thought that I was going to burst into tears as the situation was so intimidating and overwhelming. Thankfully, however, I was able to compose myself. I explained our situation, reading out some of our letters on behalf of peace. Every word was translated into Arabic. The speaker nodded, smiled and answered in Arabic which was then translated into English for our benefit.

After the formal discussion, the cameras were switched off and he spoke to us in perfect English, saying he admired our courage and the help we had given the Iraqi Women's Federation.

Wednesday December 5th 1990.

According to the *Baghdad Observer*, the National Assembly Speaker, Mr Sa'di Mahdi Saleh met "wives of a number of British nationals hosted by Iraq. He reiterated Iraq's efforts aimed at achieving peace in the region and the world at large. He also said that all the problems of the Middle East could be solved by implementing President Saddam Hussein's peace plan of August 12th."

The international news, for its part, told us that Iraq had accepted Bush's offer and that US diplomats at the UN had proposed an International Middle East peace conference.

We were told that our next meeting would be with President Saddam Hussein. This was a daunting prospect, but what we—normal, apolitical women—had achieved so far made us very proud. We were glad that we had followed our hearts, whatever the outcome would be.

The men had been allowed back, and we were very busy. There was lots going on, but exactly what it entailed was not clear. We sat and discussed the prospect of meeting with Saddam Hussein. The dates were yet to be arranged through the Iraqi diplomats. We still held out for receiving a gold watch with Saddam's face on it!

Thursday December 6th 1990.

Extraordinary news. Saddam said he was prepared to allow all hostages to leave Iraq and Kuwait! We jumped up and down with excitement and total disbelief, but realised we should react with caution after four months of false hopes.

All the men started arriving from all the various installations carrying their black bin liners. We recognised the military men; the British Liaison team taken from Ahmadi in Kuwait, many of whom we thought had been executed. The hotel lobby was full of excitement and strong emotions. The men were tired, thin and gaunt after their experience, but grateful to be alive. Everyone was desperate to tell stories of their experiences over the past four months. It was a huge reunion.

The necessary documentation, such as passports and exit papers, would take a few days to process, so we weren't quite home yet.

Monday December 10th 1990.

The news reported that more than five hundred Westerners, including a hundred Britons, flew out of Baghdad. We were the first to leave after President Saddam Hussein's order that we should all be home for Christmas. A chartered Iraqi jumbo jet had been arranged for us, the former human shields. Two other Iraqi aircraft went to Kuwait to pick up the people in hiding. There were about four hundred and fifty Britons in all. Some of the Western hostages arrived in Rome, as a hundred and seventy six of them were Italian.

We were all elated to know that the men were to be released. We joked that Saddam had listened to our pleas and that perhaps we had made a difference, although we would never really know what convinced him to change his mind and release the people who were effectively protecting his country from war.

One of the release conditions was that we had to fly out of Iraq on a US-chartered Iraqi Airways Boeing 747 Aircraft, as Iraqi airspace was closed because of the impending war. Iraq had refused permission for the British Airways plane to land on Iraqi soil.

The thought of travelling on an Iraqi aircraft made my stomach churn.

After lots of confusion, we were eventually loaded onto buses from the Mansour Melia Hotel in Baghdad and driven to Saddam International Airport. Most of the men sat quietly on the buses, collecting their thoughts and reliving their fears of the last four months. At the airport we were met by the British Ambassador, who said a few brief words.

Finally, we boarded the Frankfurt-bound plane. Chris and I held hands as we sat next to each other. Sarah and John sat close by. The men were still suspicious of where and how our journey would end. They wondered if this was Saddam's last effort to oppose Margaret Thatcher, who still maintained that the hostages' plight would not stop military action. She had stressed that the military option could not be ruled out in the Gulf and that the taking of hostages must not be allowed to determine how to act against a dictator like Saddam Hussein.

The journey seemed to last an eternity. The flight was nerve-wracking. I was sure that the Iraqi pilot had not flown a plane since the international embargo had stopped almost all international flights from Iraq! As we approached Frankfurt Airport, the pilot hovered in the sky and attempted to land. For reasons unknown, we descended suddenly at a speed that scared us all and made me feel sick. Just as suddenly, we ascended steeply back up into the sky. The pilot made three terrifying attempts to land. We were convinced that he was going to crash the plane, just when we were so close to being free. I gripped Chris' hand tightly each time we swooped down. Gasps of shock and screams were audible all around us. I prayed that this wouldn't be the end. Maybe this had been Saddam's plan; to give false hope only to avenge the West by killing us all on an Iraqi 747. The smell of fear and sweat from our bodies was intoxicating as the pilot hovered in the sky before descending once again. I closed my eyes and held Chris' hand while he whispered that he loved me and we would be fine.

Once more we descended. It seemed far too fast, just like the time before, but now there was an almighty thump and we all fell forward with the impact as the plane touched down. It sped across the runway, apparently unable to stop. Thankfully, the plane eventually ground to a halt and we had made it to Frankfurt International Airport alive and in one piece.

Thank you, God, I thought, *for giving us a second chance!*

In the airport, we were escorted to an area closed off to the public. We were all tired and gaunt after the flight from hell. Drinks and food were provided during our four hour wait and we were free to reflect on the recent events. The men were still in shock and clearly confused, understandably so after what they had been through in Iraq. Some of the men were on a high, but I suspected that they were destined for a fall when reality set in.

Finally we boarded a British airways 767 plane to freedom, complete with four hundred quarter bottles of champagne, BA gift packs and tracksuits. The experience seemed unreal as the champagne flowed freely. Journalists were also part of the package, and they were ready to talk to anyone about their experience in Iraq. Some, especially those who had gone into hiding in Kuwait, were desperate to talk after having spent so many months in isolation.

Chris and I sat quietly and talked about our future plans. Chris was still trying to come to terms with the past months, while the bubbles from the champagne went straight to my head! We arrived at London Heathrow one and a half hours later. As the BA flight landed on British soil, the screams and cheers of relief were tremendous. I started to cry.

Chris carried his black bin liner plus his bag from BA as we were escorted through the airport and into an area surrounded by flashing cameras. There, waiting in the crowds, were our families. We had a very emotional reunion. We had been very fortunate to have survived the crisis in Kuwait and Iraq.

In my heart, I believe God wanted us to survive. For whatever reason, we had been given a second chance. Now, we had to come to terms with what had happened and get on with our lives. Hopefully we had learned from the experience and were better people for it.

One day, our memories of internments in prison camps, hotels and military installations in Iraq would be ghosts from our past.

Chris and I decided to get married in the spring or early summer. Our shared experience, which was difficult for anyone else to understand, had brought us closer together. We had shared moments of terror, but also many of laughter. We were very fortunate. Some families had a very difficult time adjusting. Older men were concerned about their families, payments for mortgages and schooling. All the bank accounts in Kuwait had been frozen with war pending in the Gulf, so many lives were totally destroyed. The British government granted hostages an emergency loan of five hundred pounds, repayable once paid employment had begun.

Depression became a major problem for those who had survived. It was suggested that hostages should have a medical examination and see a psychiatrist to evaluate the degree of mental pain and anguish they had suffered. Jay said he would visit all the psychiatrists and behave as mental as they wanted if it meant he would get compensation for the hell he had endured. Unfortunately, he died before any payment was made.

The Ministry of Defence interviewed Chris and asked him about the various camps he had been held in. They wanted any information he could provide about weapons and the Iraqi military. The British government asked all hostages to complete claim forms. They put people into various categories, using criteria such as contractual losses, mental pain and anguish and loss of property. The money was to be paid in interim payments once the forms had been vetted and approved by the Foreign Office.

The United Nations agreed to Iraq selling volumes of oil for medical provisions, with a percentage of the money going to the United Nations fund to compensate hostages. This process continued for up to eight years. By then, most hostages had rebuilt their lives and any form of payment received was a bonus.

What happened next

Chris and I lived with my parents for a year. We both had moments of depression, but our families were wonderful in helping us come to terms with the ordeal. Chris went on the dole while he desperately sought work. Most employers reacted with horror when he mentioned where he had been for the last six months, convinced he must somehow be mentally deranged. Chris refused to see a psychiatrist, as he was concerned that it would go against him when trying to find work and wouldn't look too encouraging to a future employer.

As the threat of military action against the Iraqi regime became inevitable, all we could do was observe from afar.

In January 1991, a coalition of twenty eight nations, led by the Americans and including Britain, Egypt and France, began an air offensive that lasted six weeks. During the ground war, the two hundred thousand or so Iraqi forces retreated, leading to the expulsion of the Iraqi forces from Kuwait and causing a huge humanitarian crisis. There were millions of refugees and devastating environmental damage from the blown up oil wells and oil spillage that destroyed large areas in Kuwait. The pollution from the smoke caused respiratory problems for those still in Kuwait but eventually the small country would rebuild its infrastructure and restore its former glory.

Chris had odd jobs for a while. He helped my brother with his building company doing some labouring, and my brother-in-law with his glazing company. It was a far cry from what we had left behind—the sunshine and wonderful lifestyle—but at least we had each other. We were madly in love and had plans to travel again.

We wanted a small wedding, just close family and friends in our Irish family priest's flat. We had the official Catholic ceremony in the church, but a private wedding service at the altar in Father Breen's home. It was a very simple service with my small niece, Charlotte, as a flower girl and a tape playing *Ave Maria* sung by nuns at Westminster Cathedral. My wedding dress was made the week before, a simple white, calf-length dress. Emotions ran high and in some respects it was more like a funeral than a happy wedding day! Everyone cried as they reflected on the events of the past year and what Chris and I had endured. I cried throughout the service, too. Seeing everyone else in tears made it almost impossible for me to compose myself.

Afterwards, we had a fantastic celebration in a hotel and continued until late at my parents' house. We were lucky to be alive and together; now we had to be strong and live our lives from this new beginning.

We did eventually have a lucky break. Chris managed to get a hotel manager job near Rutland. We rented a twee 100-year-old cottage and I worked locally in a nursing home. We both desperately wanted to travel overseas again, and after many setbacks, God smiled down on us once more. After an interview in Edinburgh, we found ourselves en route to a country called Qatar in the Middle East! Chris had secured the position of resident manager for a hotel in Doha.

Needless to say, our families were apprehensive about us travelling back to the region. We managed to convince them that as Qatar was a small peninsula and virtually unheard of, we should be safe and far enough away from Iraq or Kuwait. Well away from any conflict!

We arrived in Qatar in September 1993. The small country is located half way down the Gulf, some 11,437 square kilometres in size, including a number of islands in the coastal waters. During the Gulf war in 1991, Qatar was part of the Allied Coalition and the Coalition's high tech-command centre was just outside the capital of Doha. The world's media was also based there. A formal agreement still exists to allow the US to use the huge Al-Udeid Air Base, from where the first raids of the Gulf War were launched. We considered the country safe, as only the main Gulf countries— Saudi Arabia, Kuwait and Bahrain—appeared to be involved in the Gulf war. Most people were not even aware of Qatar. Qatar was the first Gulf Arab country to reopen ties with Iraq after its invasion of Kuwait.

I still remember our journey and the evening we arrived in Qatar vividly. As we approached the terminal, the waft of dry heat on our skin was so welcoming. We listened to the Arabic voices all around us and recognised the unmistakeable scent of *bokhor*, the sweet smelling agar wood, burned as a sign of Arabic hospitality. It is a mix of white musk, sandalwood oil, ambergris, mystica and rose oil, and is usually impregnated on the ladies' *abayas*. The familiar wafts of smoke from the incense burners brought back fond memories of Kuwait. We were both excited but a little apprehensive.

We were met at the airport and driven in a limousine to the hotel to start our new life. We telephoned home to say all was well. The next chapter in our lives had begun.

After Chris' two year contract was over, we had become so comfortable we decided to stay a little longer and eventually the two years turned into twelve! The lifestyle and the sunshine were addictive and life was good. People are generally much happier when the sun shines almost daily. Crime is virtually unheard of in Qatar and we felt so safe—we were even able to leave cars unlocked.

At first it was hard to understand the local censorship department, responsible for censoring local publications and local and foreign artistic productions. They had to approve the publication and circulation of printed matter such as magazines. These were usually imported from Europe and were expensive because of their weight. Most pages were defaced by a black marker pen to cover any cleavage, arms or legs, so they were generally not worth buying. Before satellite TV, television was censored, too. Half way through a programme, a huge star would appear in the centre of the screen if it contained any form of embrace, kissing or any sensual activity at all. Of course, once the picture returned to the screen you had missed the plot! When *Baywatch* appeared on television it was exciting to see if the censorship department missed any parts!

Although Qatar is not classed as a dry state, alcohol was not readily available in hotels or restaurants when we first arrived. Non-Muslims had a permit to buy a hundred pound allowance of alcohol per month, for private consumption. Over time, these regulations have changed. Alcohol is now freely available in hotels, restaurants, and private parties for non-Muslims. We do, however, respect the values of a Muslim country and its people, so we abide by the rules and dress conservatively in public.

I have had various jobs, including working for airlines, as a dental nurse, a school nurse and even teaching English as a foreign language to children.

To our delight, Chris moved jobs to one of the oil companies as a General Services Manager. Life was to get even better when, after a few disappointments, I fell pregnant. In August 1996, our beautiful daughter, Candida, was born in the UK. Three weeks after the birth, I arrived back in Qatar with her. Qatar is a wonderful country for bringing up a family. The local people adore children and have very strong family values. The country itself is very child-friendly and children are welcome in most establishments. At weekends, families meet at the

Corniche; a seven kilometre landscaped shoreline. It is a beautiful place to relax. These families are a mix of nationalities—Palestinians, Indians, Jordanians, Pakistani, Algerian and Egyptian—who live in apartments around the city. Grandparents, parents and children sit together on their chairs eating and talking late into the night.

After working with another oil and gas company, Chris was approached with an offer for his dream job in the hospitality business.

We have seen Qatar develop and progress over a period of time, in industry as well as economy and trade and in the recognition of the importance of environmental protection and conservation. Qatar set up a new General Tourism Authority in 2000, promoting itself as a luxury tourist destination. It focuses on the culture, tradition, heritage, education and everyday lifestyle of this part of Arabia.

Times change and the once small state of Qatar was soon recognised by everyone, not just as the home of the Al Jazeera Television Network, but also for being the command centre of US forces in the Gulf. Their headquarters operate from the Sayliyah base, fifteen kilometres from Doha.

2002

With the build up to the war with Iraq, the US Air Force started to move its military headquarters from Saudi Arabia to Qatar, as the Saudi Government refused to allow attacks to be launched on Afghanistan from Saudi soil. The stability of the Saudi royal family had been under threat from Islamic militants over the issue of allowing American military occupation of Islam's holy sites.

The preparation to close the Prince Sultan Base and relocate its central command to the Al-Udeid air base, nineteen miles south west of Doha, with its huge hangers and the longest runways in the Gulf, continued. Qatar was seen as a more stable and willing host, and since overthrowing his father in 1995, the Emir, Sheikh Hamad Bin Khalifa Al Thani, has continued to receive US backing.

So here we were, living in Qatar and waiting to see how the local residents would react to having such a huge American military presence on their soil, involved with the US "War On Terror".

In December, the US military exercise began in Qatar. US and British troops massed throughout the region, under the instructions of General Tommy Franks, commander of the US forces in the Gulf, from the As-Sayliyah army base. Life in Qatar was changing. There was the constant noise from the military aircraft flying overhead. Even the American military presence in the shopping malls was obvious, as they were always in groups of six or more with the standard short back and sides haircut. Some looked so young and unaware of what lay in store for them. They were allowed to stay in local hotels at weekends to get away from the base for some R&R. When they arrived, we decided not to visit the beach at weekends. We had been advised to keep a low profile with the build-up to war in Iraq, avoiding shopping malls, cinemas and any large gatherings of Westerners. It brought back memories of years before in Kuwait and I was scared and aware of how quickly situations can escalate out of control. You could feel the increasing tension. I started to question road rage, which is a normal part of driving in Qatar. As the forces moved in, I felt vulnerable and intimidated. There were isolated incidents, but generally life went on as normal. The reaction to any unpleasant incidents was that of the typical British stiff upper lip. We realised that it was important not to cause unnecessary anguish, which could develop into mass hysteria and panic. But the American school's security was impossible to by-pass as exits were blocked, ID passes were issued to students and staff and a strong armed police presence was established. For the English-speaking school attended by the majority of British children, along with many other nationalities, including children from some of the prominent Qatari families, security consisted of a couple of unarmed men in security uniforms, who would pose no threat in the event of conflict.

On a number of occasions, after leaving Candida in her classroom I sat in the car observing suspicious looking characters sitting outside the school gates. A few times, I also wrote down their car registrations and gave them to the school office. At the time, everybody felt uncomfortable with the current political situation and the topic of increasing the security in and around the school was a major issue. I'm sure they just thought I was an over-protective mother who was paranoid because of our past experiences. A lot of the expatriates appeared not to be too concerned. Paranoid or not, Chris and I were well aware of how situations can develop where you have absolutely no control. Politically, things were becoming much tenser and we decided to keep Candida at home for one week until a police presence was visible at the school. Eventually, after various ministries were contacted, we received armed police presence at the various exit gates.

The US President George Bush and Iraq continued to disagree about the weapons of mass destruction. The Arab states said that UN must be given more time. Some Arab editorials said Washington was determined to wage war, whatever the outcome. It was claimed that they had an eye on the Iraqis' wealth and were using Iraq's alleged possession of weapons as a pretext.

Again, our families telephoned, concerned for our safety. Having lived through our experience during the Gulf War in 1991, they understood how delicate the situation was and how quickly the situation could spin out of control. We tried to reassure them and promised that if we felt unable to cope, or at the first sign of a threat towards us as a family, we would leave immediately.

We received warnings from the British Embassy wardens when any anti-war marches were taking place. They were usually held on the Corniche on Friday afternoons, with some anti-Western feeling. Sometimes they consisted of hundreds of youths pumped high with adrenaline, so it was suggested that, during these times, we should maintain a low profile. Generally, however, they were peaceful protests with a high police presence.

February.

Despite being a tiny Gulf Arab State, Qatar was expected to become a main launch pad for any US strike on Iraq. American F-117A Stealth bombers were now in Qatar and most likely to be the first aircraft to launch the war.

March.

The British Embassy closed the English School, emphasising that this was not in response to a specific threat, and that they did not want to spread alarm. In the circumstances, the school believed that it would be prudent to close until further notice.

The British Embassy also issued warnings for the British community to maintain a low profile and avoid large gatherings in hotels and shopping malls. We had been advised to change our daily routes and to be observant.

It was only natural to feel frightened. Usually, I would travel with my Arabic friends to the malls. Life carried on as normally as possible, but I spent a lot of time at home. The military aircraft travelled over our home at such speed the noise was deafening. We often ran up to the roof to see the aircraft flying overhead.

The Foreign Office updated its travel advice for Qatar, saying: "Military action in Iraq is underway. There is an increased threat to British nationals in neighbouring countries. The threat to British individuals and organisations from terrorism is high. Terrorist attacks in the region could involve the use of chemical and biological materials. There is a risk of the use of chemical and biological weapons by Iraq. Qatar might be affected.

People are advised not to make any non-essential travel (excluding passengers in transit, providing they do not break their journey) to Qatar. In the event of military action, it is possible that Qatar airspace will be closed temporarily until the authorities review the situation. If already in Qatar, you should maintain a high level of vigilance and consider whether your presence and that of your dependants is essential. There may be a short-term disruption to commercial flights as a result of military action. The Embassy in Qatar has authorised the voluntary departure of the dependants of its staff, and also the non-essential staff that want to leave. Although no incidents have occurred which directly affected British nationals, we believe that Qatar, in common with the entire Gulf region, is a place where the threat to British individuals and organisations from terrorism is now high. It will rise further with military action in Iraq. In the event of a chemical or biological incident, you should follow the instructions of the local authorities and emergency services. You should ensure in advance that you are familiar with contact details for the emergency services and with contingency plans prepared by them for the general public."

Qatar became the media centre for the international press and television crews. Whilst most Gulf regions were severely affected by the political situation in Iraq, Qatar was finding it almost impossible to provide enough hotel rooms. Business was booming because of the American command centre that hosted press meetings throughout the conflict.

The European Tour Qatar Masters Golf tournament was to take place in Doha in early March and, of course, the media were following the event. Some professional golfers decided not to venture into Qatar following the advice from the Foreign Office, and lack of insurance cover in the event of any terrorist activity. Having said that, many famous names in the golf circuit decided to attend. Thankfully, the tournament went ahead as planned and was a huge success. Life in Qatar remained pretty normal, but listening to news broadcasts around the world you would have thought that we were all hiding in bunkers!

It was difficult to explain to the family why we were still in Qatar. We told them that Chris had a lot of responsibilities at work. We had made Qatar our home; Candida had known no other. Her school and friends were here. If we felt under any direct threat, then of course Candida's safety would come first and we would leave at once.

Fortunately, the school holidays coincided with conflict in Iraq. Air strikes started overnight around Baghdad as the coalition forces prepared to invade the Iraqi capital. We stayed in and prayed for an end to the horrid suffering on both sides. We sat in the villa watching the coverage of "War on Terror", switching from channel to channel. Our Arabic friends called and told us to switch to the Al Jazeera channel.

The Al Jazeera Channel was established in 1996 with the purpose of providing the Arab world an alternative news source to the frequently watched CNN and BBC. Al Jazeera is credited with revolutionising public opinion and the media in the Arab world by virtue of its resoluteness to maintaining its independence from the censor.

We listened and followed the developments. The television was on constantly, as we were unable to sleep. Like so many, I was opposed to the war and continued to hope that they could reach another end to the political situation. The pain and suffering on both sides was devastating.

April 2003.

The news in April informed us that despite evidence of terrorists' plans to attack Western targets linked to Iraq, the Foreign Office relaxed travel warnings against travelling to Kuwait, Bahrain, Saudi Arabia, Syria, Israel, Jordan and Qatar. There remained a high threat to British individuals and organisations in the region. Developments in Iraq and in the Middle East peace plans continued to have an impact on public opinion in the region, so we would have to maintain a very high level of vigilance in public places.

Everyone tried to carry on as normal and some events continued as planned. Pavarotti came to Doha and put on a spectacular show, followed by the Bolshevik Ballet. The situation in Iraq continued; although President Saddam Hussein was no longer in power, the bitter fighting destabilised the region.

November 2003.

The Foreign Office continued to update travel advice to Qatar, saying that there was a high threat from terrorism, and that Westerners should review their security arrangements carefully, remaining especially vigilant in public places.

We were safe but always vigilant as the tension in the region mounted. There was a threat from Al Qaeda, but that risk was everywhere, including London and New York. We remained in Qatar. It still held many opportunities for us. But foreign residents had to accept that political unrest would continue for many years to come, and the Foreign Office would continue to issue travel warnings to the region. I believed that fate would intervene when our time was up. For now, we lived life to the full and prayed for peace.

<u>December 2003.</u>

Qatar had been a very welcoming home from home for my family. We had many friends of all nationalities, which I felt was a way forward. It was a wonderful experience for Candida to live and feel part of a different culture. It was very educational; children grow up with a better understanding of other cultures, hopefully dissolving the bitterness that is so common in those with little understanding of other ethnicities.

Years before, we experienced an abrupt end to our time in Kuwait, having been "guests" of President Saddam Hussein, but we had learned some special lessons in life and I hoped we were better people for it. We looked at life very differently, did not suffer fools gladly and, hopefully, had the wisdom to teach our daughter Candida that one cannot generalise about nations and that one should treat people with respect, whatever their creed or culture.

Saturday 19th March 2005.

Our worst fear became reality. A major incident had happened.

This evening, Chris was out at a business dinner. He called me at about half past eight to say that a bomb had exploded at the Doha Players Theatre, opposite our daughter's school. The information was sketchy and there was no confirmation about what had caused the explosion. Some said it could be a gas explosion. The BBC reported that a British school in Doha had been damaged by a car bomb. Al Jazeera television reported that a suicide bomber had driven into the Doha Players Theatre during an amateur performance of Shakespeare's *Twelfth Night*. The coverage showed fire raging at the scene. The West End hall of the theatre was reduced to ashes. That part of the theatre, which was used for snacks and drinks during the intermission, was usually full of theatregoers. The previous night's intermission had been earlier, so most had already returned to the auditorium at the time of the explosion and about a hundred people escaped quickly. The explosion's impact blew windows and doors out of the teachers' accommodation at the school and shocked and terrified teachers ran for cover. The loud explosion was heard and tremors felt over much of Doha. Many injuries were caused by flying glass and homes and buildings within a wide radius suffered severe damage.

Sky News also covered the explosion. I sat crying, switching from channel to channel. The live pictures on Al Jazeera showed the carnage and the school walls. I prayed that there were few casualties, but looking at the television coverage it seemed that that would have been a miracle. Cars parked outside the theatre were badly damaged and some were on fire. Car parts and railings had been blown through the air.

Inevitably, there were casualties. One British man was killed, as well as the suicide bomber. The theatre had been a very popular meeting place and had had frequent visitors, supporting the amateur actors. It was renowned for its fantastic pantomimes, with children booking a full house.

By now, Candida had woken up.

"What happened, Mum?" she asked, seeing my distress. There was little point avoiding telling her the truth, as the whole expat community would be talking about the incident, which had also affected her school. As the news broke, my mobile immediately started ringing, as did my house-phone. Friends wanted to check that we were home and not at the theatre. Arabic friends also called to see if we were safe. They were deeply upset by what had happened. Our Qatari friends were very apologetic. Concerned family called to see if we were okay after seeing the news in the UK.

Doha is a small community with about five thousand British expats, almost like a village. Everyone looks out for one another and the grapevine is a great source of information. Chris phoned constantly to give me updates.

The school had an effective system called the Emergency Telephone Tree; a rapid method of communicating with a large number of people. Each class elects a "class mum" who is the contact point when the school needs to pass important information to all the parents as quickly as possible. The details of each parent are compiled in a tree system for each class, with the class mum at the top. In emergencies, each parent is responsible for contacting the parents directly below them on the class tree and passing on the message. Today, the message was that school was closed until further notice. Wardens from the British Embassy would contact residents via e-mail with updated information.

The next day would have been a non-uniform day and cake bake sale. We had a kitchen full of cakes! The money raised from cakes was to have been for the disadvantaged children supported by the school's chosen charity, "Hope and Homes for Children", an international charity organisation working with children who have been abandoned as a result of war or other disasters throughout Africa and Eastern Europe.

I was shocked by what had taken place and unsure of what to expect for the coming weeks. I was scared and saddened for Qatar. It had been our home for the past twelve years and was a beautiful, safe country. This would change everything. John, my brother, called from Ireland, as did some good friends who had left Qatar. Everyone's concern made me even more nervous.

We received information regarding the bomb attack from the British Embassy via e-mail:

A suicide bomb attack occurred at 9.15 local time on 19th March 2005 outside the Doha Players' Theatre, Doha. I want to brief you about this event, consequences for your security and some general security tips to help you better protect yourself. Please bring this to the attention of your fellow UK nationals.

One British national was killed and at least 12 people of various nationalities were injured in the blast, outside the Doha Players' Theatre. The investigation into this attack continues by the Qatari Authorities. We are staying in close contact with them and we are also taking advice from London on the current security threat levels.

We have requested that the Qatari Authorities increase the Police presence around British Embassy sponsored schools and British institutions. The English School informed us they are aiming to re-open during the week of 10 April.

We assess that there continues to be a high threat from terrorism against Western, including British, interests in Qatar. As we have seen, attacks could be indiscriminate and against civilian targets. You should follow news reports and be alert to regional developments.

In this period of increased concern, you should take sensible precautions for your personal safety and avoid public gatherings and demonstrations.

It is advisable that you should review your security arrangements carefully.

You should remain vigilant, particularly in public places.

Further advice is available on the FCO web-site.

Further updates were sent. Hamad Hospital was offering psychological support and debriefing for people who were in the theatre at the time of the bombing. The attack against Doha Players Theatre was condemned by Qatari citizens. The attack was against all religious principles. Arab and international leaders also condemned the bombing. The six nation Gulf Co-operation Council confirmed its rejection of all criminal and terrorists acts. Newspapers reported that the bomber had been identified as an Egyptian national and investigations were underway.

Monday 21st March 2005.

A peaceful rally took place following *Asr* (afternoon) prayers, to condemn the suicide car bomb attack. The "Rally of Indignation" invited all Doha residents to join together to express rejection of the criminal act that injured innocent people, including children. The British Embassy, however, advised that participation in this event went against their general advice and that British Nationals should continue to keep away from public events and functions of this nature.

Qatar had always been a safe haven and the Qatari people had expressed their deep sorrow over the incident. Four thousand people joined the rally to protest against it, including senior officials, ministers, scholars, prominent businessmen, members of the Central Municipal Council, school children and a number of Western expatriates. Qatar, although a small peninsula, prides itself on its security and had never experienced suicide bombings before.

I was devastated that something like this could happen here. After living in this region for the past twelve years, I could only hope it would remain an isolated case and that Qatar would remain safe and prosperous.

The memories of our experience during the 1991 Gulf war made us more nervous, as we knew how these situations escalate out of control. The teachers at Candida's school were seriously shaken, but had sustained no physical injuries because blast proof film had been applied to every window in the school. The teachers were moved to other accommodation while the headmaster stayed on site. The school had sustained considerable damage and remained closed. Almost every window was blown out of the staff quarters, the main hall and other areas around the school. Debris from the suicide bomber's car and remnants of the theatre were scattered over parts of the school grounds.

Chris visited the school the morning following the blast as a member of the Board of School Governors. He was deeply upset. He couldn't help but imagine how it would have been if the children had been caught up in the aftermath. A window in our daughter's classroom had blown out. As the Easter break was due, the school would clean up then, and hopefully be operational again for next term. Members of the Anti-Terrorist Branch, Special Branch and Bomb Squad from London had been at the school site helping the Qatari Authorities with the investigation. Advice had been offered on reviewing security around the school perimeter. During the school closure, concrete blocks would be arranged around the perimeter wall, blocking off many of the car parking bays. When it re-opened, police vehicles would be stationed at the four corners of the school and the main gate. Staff requested police cover for out of school hours. There would be armed police day and night. Prior to the opening of the school on the tenth of April, the Qatari police would thoroughly check the school site.

We kept a low profile in the first few days. Friends gathered together with children, trying to occupy and keep them entertained for the extended Easter break. After a few days, everything appeared to be returning to normal. We all got on with business as usual. Obviously, the main topic of conversation was the Doha Players. Most people knew somebody who had been there that evening.

The school's headmaster worked tirelessly with the Qatari Authorities to get the school up and running in time for the new term. He was also responsible for maintaining contact with concerned parents via the school's web-site. The Chairman of the Board of Governors established contact and communication with the Board members, some of whose children were students at the school.

Chris and I had very mixed feelings about our daughter returning to the school. It was very much a catch 22 situation: Do we pack up and go? Where would we go? Imagine if this happened in London; would you leave your house, cats, dog, work and travel elsewhere? We felt we were sensible, practical people who would not put our daughter's well-being at risk. Considering all the options, we reviewed the situation and decided we would stay. Security had been increased all over the country. Worrying is like a rocking chair; you rock backwards and forwards but go nowhere.

3rd April 2005.

Pope John Paul II passed away. Saddened and emotional, as Roman Catholics we wanted to say good-bye and pay our respects to a remarkable man. The Catholic Church of our Lady of The Rosary had decided to step up security around the perimeter of the parish centre. Unfortunately, the church was a target as many Westerners, Christian Arabs and Asians met there for services. We drove to the church in the morning. It was unnerving to see the concrete bollards surrounding the perimeter of the outer wall. We wanted to sign the Condolence book and attend mass. My little girl clutched her prayer book and I prayed that we would be kept safe and that we were making the right decision in staying. We wrote our messages hoping for peace and love in the world, just as John Paul prayed for all his life.

Sunday 10th April 2005.

I had many sleepless nights about our daughter returning to school. Finally the day arrived. Chris suggested that perhaps she could miss the first day; he had a gut feeling that something might happen. The alarm rang at six in the morning after a very disturbed sleep. Candida was a little nervous and very aware at what had happened so close to her school, but she was also excited about seeing her friends.

School starts at half past seven in Qatar and finishes at one because of the hot climate. As we arrived, I noticed the school's perimeter walls ringed with concrete bollards for additional security. Armed police, some in their cars, were at each gate. There were five police vehicles. Anxious parents walked their children to their classrooms. The obvious police presence made me feel more comfortable and reassured me about the children's and teachers' safety. Blast proof film had been put on all windows, including the staff accommodation and the height of the security fence surrounding the entire perimeter of had been increased. A hotline connection to authorities for emergency situations was also to be installed and further security measures were to be enforced.

On British Embassy advice, buses would no longer be allowed into the school site. Staff were to be trained in security procedures by an external consultant. Installation of anti-ram bars at all other gates had been implemented. Closed circuit TV cameras were to be fitted around the perimeter walls and gates, and gates that were not required for access and presented a security risk were to be bricked up. There would be more rigorous security procedures for visitors entering during school hours.

Candida's first day went without incident. She was excited to be with her friends, although not all children turned up for school.

Monday 11th April 2005.

At school in the morning, we had to walk past a police officer standing outside Candida's access gate with his machine gun. I had felt guilty and afraid as I hoped and prayed that all the children would be safe. We were reviewing our options and prayed that Qatar would continue to strive for democracy. Thinking of all that had happened in the past few years, it was difficult to imagine life being normal. But life went on. Qatar strove continuously to establish and develop close ties with all peace-loving countries. The Gulf region continued to face unexpected challenges and concerns.

In time, God willing, through closer relations, we can all live in peace.\

About the Author

Caroline Hughes Myers was born into an Irish family in the United Kingdom, where she grew up, completed her education and trained to be a nurse.

When the opportunity arose, Caroline seized the chance to make an exciting new start by moving to Kuwait in the late 1980s, to take up a managerial position in a prestigious department store. In Kuwait, she met her partner and future husband, Chris.

Caroline and Chris were seized, among thousands of other foreign nationals, when Iraq invaded Kuwait in 1990. They were to become "human shields" in Saddam Hussein's attempts to evade war. Throughout her ordeal, Caroline kept a daily record of events, recording her hopes, fears and dreams for the future. Fortunately, both she and Chris survived their period of captivity, and returned after some months to the United Kingdom where they were married.

Caroline and Chris currently reside in Doha, Qatar, with their daughter Candida, where Caroline is employed as the Advertising Manager for a women's publication that is distributed across the Arab Gulf. She is also a very busy wife and mother and is active in local fundraising activities. This is her first book.

www.ingramcontent.com/pod-product-compliance
Lightning Source LLC
Chambersburg PA
CBHW031320290526
45784CB00014B/318